'Through careful attention to the text and a clear spiritual eye, Wallace Benn brings us around the table with Christ on that final night he spent with his disciples. Here our soul feasts.'

Kent Hughes, College Church, Wheaton, USA.

'The greatest need of the Christian church, worldwide, is a return to real Bible teaching. In *The Last Word*, we have been given a grand model, by one of today's most respected Bible teachers.'

Richard Bewes, All Souls Church, London.

'A rich feast of Bible teaching on some vitally relevant chapters of John's Gospel.'

Steve Gaukroger, Gold Hill Baptist Church,
Chalfont St Peter, Buckinghamshire, England.

'Blending biblical insight with practical application, this moving study of Jesus' love for his people will warm your heart, instruct your faith and deepen your devotion.'

David Jackman, Proclamation Trust, London.

THE LAST WORD

Wallace Benn

Christian Focus Publications

Over the years I have collected quotations, several of which I have included in this book. Unfortunately, I am not able to remember where I read or heard some of them. Also would you please note that, unless otherwise stated, scripture references are from the Gospel of John.

Published by
Christian Focus Publications Ltd
Geanies House, Fearn, Ross-shire,
IV20 1TW, Scotland, Great Britain.

Printed and bound in Great Britain by
Cox & Wyman Ltd, Reading, Berkshire

Cover design by Keith Jackson
Cover illustration by Patricia Donnelly

Contents

For Lindsay,
Jessica and James
without whose love, help, prayer and encouragement
these pages would never have been written.

With special thanks to
New Horizon, St. Helen's Partnership,
and especially to the Staff Team, Elders and
Congregation of St. Peter's, Harold Wood,
amongst whom these chapters took shape.
You have helped in so many ways.

Introduction

I well remember the last conversation that I had with my mother before she died. I could never forget it. We said to one another all the things we wanted to say, words of love and encouragement. And my mother, sensing that her life was slipping away, with that unspoken admission between the two of us, told me the things that she wanted me to carry out, the things that were important to her. But more than that, she told me to keep going and not to get discouraged, to look constantly to the Holy Spirit for help and to seek the glory of God. She reminded me that work for him is never wasted and is eternal in its consequences.

You can imagine how much that conversation has meant to me.

In John 13-17 there is a record of the final words of Jesus to the Twelve just before his arrest which resulted in his death. Though some post-resurrection words of Jesus are recorded for us elsewhere in the Four Gospels, they are few. John, in telling what was said in the Upper Room, effectively gives us the last words of Jesus. He fills out the details of what Jesus said in a way that is not paralleled in the other Gospels and shows, in a marvellous manner that is precious beyond words, the mind of Christ before he went to the Cross.

Here is what John Stott calls 'the inner sanctuary' of the New Testament. It is precious territory indeed, and is John's equivalent of Philippians 2:5-11. In truth, that passage is a wonderful commentary on these chapters in John's Gospel. Alec Motyer writes of the passage in

Philippians that it 'uniquely unfolds the Cross as seen through the eyes of the Crucified ... (it is) very holy ground indeed'.[1] Much the same could be said of John's Upper Room discourse.

As the final words of Jesus, the essence of all that he wanted his disciples to know, these chapters need to be taken very seriously by every Christian.

They are full of pathos and poignancy. But much more than that! In these chapters we have the love of Christ displayed and explained. We have rich encouragement for bewildered Christians. We have the assurance of the on-going love of Jesus for those who are his, and the promise of his abiding presence with them by the Holy Spirit. We have an encouragement for and in the task that lies ahead. We have a job to do and the promise of strength to do it in. We are, in short, loved with a love that will never fail us.

These chapters clear the head and warm the heart about what Jesus wants of his disciples. Furthermore they are the basis of much of the rest of the New Testament's teaching on a number of key issues.

Take, for example, what the New Testament teaches about the work of the Holy Spirit. Much of the later teaching on gifts will be misunderstood if the teaching of Jesus in these chapters is not fully grasped. Much, too, will be missed of the Spirit's precious work in the believer. If we don't wish to be the poorer we need to pay attention to these chapters!

There is so much of encouragement and challenge.

Why does Christian living sometimes descend into loveless duty? The answer lies here!

---

1. Alec Motyer, *The Message of Philippians*, IVP, 1984.

Why are some believers paralysed with unanswered questions? The answer lies here!

Why is the church often sidetracked from what Jesus wants it to have as its priorities? The answer lies here!

Why do some Christians seem powerless and discouraged? The answer lies here!

What is the key to keeping sweet in our Christian life, and being fruitful for Jesus? The answer lies here!

What encouragement does my Saviour want me to take to heart? The answer lies here!

I hope by now that you will be feeling excited about these chapters! They are crucial for healthy Christian living!

They offer more than all this, however. If you are a seeker after the truth, attracted to, but not yet convinced by, the Christian faith and want a peep inside to see what it is all about, then you will find plenty to ponder in these chapters. You can look over the shoulders of those first apostles and listen to Jesus speaking to his friends about his death, its meaning and its purpose, about why it is so important and what it will make possible.

There are two other things to mention by way of introduction.

First, notice that chapter 12 of John's Gospel describes a change of focus in the ministry of Jesus. Up till then it was largely public ministry, but John reminds us in 13:1 that the focus has now changed from public proclamation to intimate discourse with his disciples. John's vocabulary changes too. The word *love* has a heavy emphasis in these next chapters.[2] This is not surprising, as Jesus is explaining his coming action of love, and calling the

2. See Leon Morris, *The Gospel According to John*, Marshall, Morgan and Scott, 1972.

disciples to follow the way of love! This will be what impresses a watching world!

Secondly, notice that, as in all the Gospels, the major section of the account is about the last week in the life of Jesus. It is not just about his ethical teaching, or his wise words, or his wonderful example, but it centres on his death! This is not the tragic end to a good life, or the inevitable end to a fatally flawed mission that went wrong at the end (cf. *Jesus Christ Superstar*). It is rather the hour of his glory! It is the reason for which he came. The death of Christ is the focus and backdrop to the dramatic and powerful actions and words of these chapters!

God has given us a precious and unparalleled account, let us then consider it carefully, that we too might see the importance of the truths recorded there.

1

The Last Demonstration

Chapter 1

A picture of the love of Jesus
(John 13:1-11)

In London, where I live, I am sure that if I were to stop individuals on the street and ask them the relevance of Christianity, they would answer something like this: 'Christianity is a bore. It simply encourages people to try hard, and deny themselves fun in life.' Many see Christianity as a system by which a person pulls up his or her own moral bootlaces and, in doing so, misses out on the very best in life. Sadly it is true that our churches can reinforce this impression, for they can be loveless and cold places.

In this chapter I intend to disprove this assertion. Hopefully we will discover how to prevent our Christian life becoming dull and legalistic, and we shall see how the Lord wants us to live. His words show the world who his followers are.

In the third part of the first verse (verse 1c), John tells us that Jesus displayed to them the full extent of his love. You may have a version which says, 'he loved them to the end'. It can be translated like that, but it is probably better to take it in a qualitative way, as does the New International Version: 'he showed them the full extent of his love'. Jesus displayed his love for them to its full degree. Or to put it another way 'he showed them the lengths to which his love would go'.

It was just before the Passover Feast. Jesus knew that the time had come for him to leave this world and go to the Father. Having loved his own who were in the world, he now showed them the full extent of his love.

² The evening meal was being served, and the devil had already prompted Judas Iscariot, son of Simon, to betray Jesus. ³Jesus knew that the Father had put all things under his power, and that he had come from God and was returning to God; ⁴so he got up from the meal, took off his outer clothing, and wrapped a towel round his waist. ⁵After that, he poured water into a basin and began to wash his disciples' feet, drying them with the towel that was wrapped round him.

⁶He came to Simon Peter, who said to him, 'Lord, are you going to wash my feet?'

⁷Jesus replied, 'You do not realise now what I am doing, but later you will understand.'

⁸'No,' said Peter, 'you shall never wash my feet.'

Jesus answered, 'Unless I wash you, you have no part with me.'

⁹'Then, Lord,' Simon Peter replied, 'not just my feet but my hands and my head as well!'

¹⁰Jesus answered, 'A person who has had a bath needs only to wash his feet; his whole body is clean. And you are clean, though not every one of you.' ¹¹For he knew who was going to betray him, and that was why he said not every one was clean (John 13:1-11).

For a full grasp of the *general* background to this display of the love of Jesus, we need to look back to some other incidents recorded by John.

First, there is growing hostility from the Pharisees, with a threat to the very life of Jesus through their plotting: 'They kept looking for Jesus, and as they stood in the temple area, they asked one another, "What do you think? Isn't he coming to the Feast at all?" But the chief priests and Pharisees had given orders that if anyone found out where Jesus was, he should report it so that they might arrest him' (11:56-57).

Second, there is the incident in the house of Martha and Mary, a home that Jesus loved to visit. Mary took a pint of pure nard, an expensive perfume, and anointed the feet of Jesus and wiped his feet with her hair. Though she was criticised, Jesus answered: 'Leave her alone ... It was meant that she should save this perfume for the day of my burial' (12:7). There was a consciousness in Jesus that the time had come, that hour for which he had entered into the world, his death on our behalf.

Third, the incident of the Gentiles seeking him acts as a trigger that makes Jesus recognise the hour (12:23). He explains this in verse 24: 'I tell you the truth, unless an ear of wheat falls to the ground and dies, it remains only a single seed. But if it dies, it produces many seeds.' In 12:32, Jesus says: 'But I, when I am lifted up from the earth, will draw all men to myself,' to which John adds, 'He said this to show the kind of death he was going to die.' How does Jesus react to the impending event? 'Right now I am storm-tossed. And what am I going to say? "Father, get me out of this?" No, this is why I came in the first place. I'll say, "Father, put your glory on display"' (12:27-28, *The Message*).

The immediate background

Having set the scene, John very carefully fills in the immediate background. It was just before the *Passover Feast*. John has already recorded that when John the Baptist saw Jesus come to him for baptism, he said, 'Look, the Lamb of God, who takes away the sin of the world!' (1:29). Every Jew knew what that meant.

The Passover was the time of remembrance of God's great Old Covenant event of deliverance and redemption from Egypt (Exodus 12). It was the event which, *par excellence*, constituted Israel as the people of God; and it was a time that was associated with a lamb. At the Exodus a pure lamb had been killed and its blood put on the doorposts, so that the angel of death might pass over those who trusted in God's command. It was, then, a remembrance of the great Passover, of God's deliverance of his people from judgment, bringing them out of Egypt, and setting them on the route to the Promised Land. It was remembered each subsequent year, in obedience to God's command; and they would eat a roasted lamb as a memorial and celebration of their deliverance.

So John very poignantly fills in the immediate background of this display of the love of Jesus which prefigured his Cross, as being the Passover event. God's timing, as ever, was immaculate.

Then the other immediate background detail is described: *the betrayal of Judas Iscariot*. 'The evening meal was being served, and the devil had already prompted Judas Iscariot, son of Simon, to betray Jesus' (13:2).

John is telling us something that is both very startling and also extremely important. Jesus' leaving of this world, by his death, to go to the Father, was the key event

that displayed his love and brought glory to God the
Father. Look at verse 31: 'When Judas had gone, Jesus
said, "Now is the Son of Man glorified and God is
glorified in him."' The crucifixion and death of the Lord
Jesus is that which supremely brings glory to Jesus, and
to God the Father as well. We might suppose that something else would bring greater glory to Jesus; but no, John
explains, very clearly, that it is the laying down of Jesus'
life which brings glory to God.

The meaning of his love

Even though his ministry was misunderstood by the
crowd who thought of him as a political Messiah, Jesus
wanted the disciples to understand his love for them. The
disciples needed to understand that the king who had been
announced in the triumphal entry into Jerusalem (12:13),
the person whom they had begun to see was the Messiah,
God's unique Son, the one for whom they had left all, was
in reality the Servant King, the Suffering Servant predict-
ed by Isaiah (Isaiah 42:1-4; 52:13-53:12).

In this acted parable of the foot-washing (for that is
what it is, an acted parable), we see displayed the inner
motive of the Cross of Christ. It is, if you like, John's
equivalent of Philippians 2.

Look how Paul, in that magnificent early Christian
hymn, says exactly the same thing as John:

> Who, being in very nature God,
>   did not consider equality with God
>   something to be grasped,
>   but made himself nothing,
>   taking the very nature of a servant,
>   being made in human likeness.

> And being found in appearance as a man,
>   he humbled himself
>   and became obedient to death –
>   even death on a cross!
> Therefore God exalted him to the highest place
>   and gave him a name that is above every name,
> that at the name of Jesus, every knee should bow
>   in heaven and on earth and under the earth,
> and every tongue confess that Jesus Christ is Lord,
>   to the glory of God the Father'
>
> (Philippians 2:6-11).

So Jesus, when the evening meal was just being served, stepped down from the table, and took a towel and placed it around him. Perhaps he waited to see if anyone else would serve the needs of the others. When they did not, he performed the job of the lowliest servant: he served them. He laid aside his outer robe and wrapped a towel around his waist (13:4).

Here is a marvellous, poignant picture of what was about to happen on the Cross; Jesus, God's Son, humbling himself and taking the very nature of a servant and being obedient unto death. He laid aside, like a garment, his rights to enjoy his place in heaven, and he came to earth to serve! Here was the Son of Man coming not to be served 'but to serve, and to give his life as a ransom for many' (Mark 10:45).

Very often, this incident in John 13 is perceived as a pattern of loving behaviour that Jesus gave to the disciples. Of course it is that! But before Jesus referred to his actions as a pattern for them to follow, he wanted them to understand the full extent of his love. 'You do not realise now what I am doing, but later you will understand,' he said to Peter (13:7).

Jesus was secure, as verse 3 tells us, in his relationship with his Father and in his Father's purposes for him, and on that basis he came to carry out the plan of God and to die on the Cross. But he also wanted his disciples to understand his love for them and to appreciate it after the events of the Passion occurred. He wanted them to understand why he had stepped down from heaven and taken the nature of a servant and been obedient to death. That is why his conversation with Simon Peter is recorded here. It is a parable within a parable.

'He came to Simon Peter, who said to him, "Lord, are you going to wash my feet?"'

'Jesus replied, "You do not realise now what I am doing, but later you will understand".'

' "No," said Peter, "you shall never wash my feet!"'

'Jesus answered, "Unless I wash you, you have no part with me " ' (13:6-8).

As has been well said: 'Peter is humble enough to see the incongruity of Jesus' actions, yet proud enough to dictate to his Master how he should behave.' There was pride here in Peter. He sees the amazing nature of Jesus stepping down and doing what none of the rest of them were prepared to do for one another. He is astonished that Jesus the King would do the lowliest act of the lowliest servant. But there is pride when he says, 'No, don't wash me! Don't do this!'

Jesus used this picture of his love to explain its reason and purpose. The reason he came to die was that his disciples would be cleansed from sin. He came so that everything which kept them from a relationship with God – their rebellion and wrongdoing – might be forgiven.

When Jesus said to Peter, 'Unless you are willing to

allow me to wash you, you have no part in me,' he intended Peter to understand that before he could serve Jesus, he needed the forgiveness and cleansing that Jesus came to procure by his death. If Peter refused it, he would have missed the point of Jesus' whole mission. Jesus wanted his disciples to understand that without cleansing from sin, accomplished by his death, they could have no part with him.

The conversation with Peter goes on to explain that not only is salvation provided for by the love of Jesus, but so also is sanctification. Look at verse 10 where Jesus said to Peter: 'A person who has had a bath needs only to wash his feet; his whole body is clean. And you are clean, though not every one of you.' In other words, Jesus said, 'I know that you have come to know me, and in the light of what I will do on the Cross, you are already clean. But I have also provided for your daily sanctification, your daily renewal. Since you have been brought into a relationship with me, and been cleansed and forgiven and before God are justified and set free, all you need is a daily washing.'

Feet are used by Jesus as a picture of his disciples' daily contact with the world. All disciples have that which brings defilement, that causes problems, that leads to sin. Jesus says, 'I have provided for that too. Though you are forgiven all your sins past, present and future, those things that daily become a cloud between you and the God who loves you, can be dealt with too. I have provided for your daily washing that you may become more like me.' All this is implied in this action of the Lord Jesus.

Jesus wanted his disciples to be secure in the fact that not only has he loved them, but he will go on loving them.

They were to be secure in his total provision for all that they needed for salvation and sanctification.

Let us apply this to ourselves. There is a key pattern here that Jesus wants us to understand. Before service for Christ, there needs to be a coming to him and a receiving from him. Before we can serve him, we need to come and receive from the hands of Jesus that which we could never gain for ourselves: God's forgiveness, God's cleansing and God's new life.

There can be no joyful service for Jesus, without first receiving from him what he came to accomplish for us. There can be no concern to glorify God, unless we have seen and experienced God's love. There will be no hardship endured in service for Christ, unless we are overjoyed with the grace and love of Christ for us. Priorities will get muddled and challenging service will be avoided. Service for Christ comes out of a deep gratitude for the love of Christ for us, and our love for him is first of all won by his love for us.

Several years ago the newspapers carried the story of two girls who were arrested and imprisoned on drug charges in Thailand. Both the Thai and British governments acknowledged the guilt of the women. But despite the acknowledged guilt, they received a royal pardon. The wonderful good news is that, despite our guilt, there is a royal pardon from God through his Son.

Some time ago, I was taking a weekend houseparty for another church. At the end of the weekend, a young man expressed his thanks to me. He said to me: 'This weekend, I have learned something very important about Christian living. My Christian life had become simply a matter of duty, and I was becoming dry and dull. My motivation to serve Jesus and my love for him was low, and I was discouraged. I have seen by the grace of God this week-end that my problem was my moving away from the Cross.'

He continued: 'When I first became a Christian, I thought constantly about the Cross, but I felt as I went on that I had to understand other things. I did need to understand other things, but I have seen this weekend that I can never safely, as a believer, move away from the foot of the Cross. I need constantly to be there, to see the greatness of his love to me, and to bask in the wonder of it. Without this, my Christian life is bound to dry up!' Wise words indeed that we neglect at our cost.

I once heard Jim Packer say: 'All problems find their solution at Calvary.' When I first heard him say this, I thought it must be an exaggeration. But the longer I have lived as a Christian, the more true I have seen his words to be. The love displayed at Calvary, and here foreshadowed in these verses by the humble foot-washing of Jesus, must cast its marvellous light over every area of our lives. Unless it does, our Christian lives will become dull and joyless. Duty which is so necessary, and the discipline that goes with it, will become lifeless and without adequate moti-vation. And our churches too will not display love.

Christianity is first of all a relationship of love to Jesus. His love for us is the only thing that can fuel our love for him, and anything we do for him. Too much Christian living is like Peter here, self-confident and proud about what we can do for Jesus. Peter needed to see, as do we, that only a grasp of the love of Christ will keep us going joyfully and prevent us making fools of ourselves!

Chapter 2

A pattern of love to follow
(John 13:12-17)

There are some humanists who admire the ethical teachings of Christianity, and want to follow them, but do not want a relationship with the Lord Jesus. They would like to see the Christian faith shorn of its faith element.

But such an outlook is wrong. In this chapter, I hope to show why.

Jesus, having then showed his disciples the full extent of his love, proceeds to give them an example of how to love. After giving the disciples a dramatic parable of his love for them, Jesus now models a pattern of love for them to follow.

'Do you understand what I have done for you?' he asked them. 'You call me "Teacher" and "Lord", and rightly so, for that is what I am. Now that I, your Lord and Teacher, have washed your feet, you also should wash one another's feet. I have set you an example that you should do as I have done for you. I tell you the truth, no servant is greater than his master, nor is the messenger greater than the one who sent him. Now that you know these things, you will be blessed if you do them.'

They called Jesus by titles of respect – 'Teacher' and 'Lord' – and he wanted them to see that they were not above their Master. The title 'Lord' can mean something like our 'Sir'. But it was a title for Jesus that had special significance for the disciples, especially after his resurrection. It is 'the name above every name' (Philippians 2:9), and was the Greek word used to translate the word Yahweh in the Septuagint (the Greek version of the Old Testament). To affirm that Jesus is Lord, is to affirm his deity and his right to be our Master. So Jesus is saying to them, 'In the light of who I am, and what I am doing for you, I have a right to call you to follow me by imitating the pattern I have given you in the foot-washing.'

It is interesting that the word translated 'messenger' or 'sent one' (verse 16) is the word *apostle*. They were not to have too high an opinion of themselves! They were the Lord's servants and as such must see that the essence of their position and calling is the privilege of imitating their Master by serving. Service is the basis of Christian ministry.

What a contrast here between the disciples, on the one

When he had finished washing their feet, he put on his clothes and returned to his place. 'Do you understand what I have done for you?' he asked them.

¹³'You call me "Teacher" and "Lord", and rightly so, for that is what I am. ¹⁴Now that I, your Lord and Teacher, have washed your feet, you also should wash one another's feet. ¹⁵I have set you an example that you should do as I have done for you. ¹⁶I tell you the truth, no servant is greater than his master, nor is a messenger greater than the one who sent him. ¹⁷Now that you know these things, you will be blessed if you do them' (John 13:12-17).

hand, jockeying for position in the Kingdom of God, alert for and concerned about their own position, power and privileges (Luke 22:24-27), and, on the other hand, the King of the Kingdom who is not above humbly washing the feet of the disciples.

Here is an example of the kind of servants he wants; not those who stand on their dignity, but those who are willing to serve humbly! Here is exemplified what real love involves. It is not primarily a feeling, but an attitude that is willing to put the interests of the object of its love first.

Jesus, in this acted parable, has shown that he loves the disciples even unto death, and therefore wants them to begin a life of love not in word but in deed.

The word *love* has become debased in our society. Often to say 'I love you' means little more than to say 'I want you to fulfil my needs'. It has become self-orientated and self-absorbed. What a challenge the pattern of love given by Jesus actually is!

To help us understand what is being taught here, let me ask six questions of the passage which I believe draw out its teaching very clearly.

1. How are we to love?

In those days, foot-washing was a courtesy offered to a guest. Remember that the streets then were not only dirty and dusty but also would have sewage in them. It was an act of kindness, if one invited someone for a meal, to arrange for a servant to wash their feet. Actually it was the task of the lowliest servant.

We have already suggested that Jesus may have waited to see if anyone would offer this service to the rest, and when no-one did, he himself did it gladly. The background against which this took place was the disciples' preoccupation with their own status in the Kingdom of God. Against this background Jesus models a different way of life for them.

The love that Jesus patterns is practical and sacrificial. It is the kind of love that considers the needs of others, and it is willing to meet those needs even when it is costly. It is all too possible to concentrate only on words of love.

But words are important. I well remember the first time that my wife told me that she loved me! But more important than that is seventeen years of displaying that love. I remember a teenager asking my wife: 'How do you know when you are in love?' Her reply initially disappointed me, but later I saw how right it was. She replied: 'I knew that I loved him when I was gladly willing to wash his dirty socks for him!'

It is all too easy to talk of loving other Christians, but it is quite another thing to have a love that is practical and sacrificial.

Too often in the church, there is a concern to have the limelight. People can be concerned, oh so concerned, about status. They want a job that is high profile and wish to be noticed and thanked and praised for what they do. We ought to encourage one another, we ought to thank one another. But why are we serving: for ourselves or for the sake of others, to the glory of God?

It is true that too often in churches people are diffident about serving and using their gifts, and are unwilling to volunteer, waiting always to be asked. In the example of Jesus we see one who was neither unwilling or hesitant about serving, nor unwilling to do that which was unpleasant. We should be no different.

I was talking to a lay assistant at a church recently who said that one of his tasks is to clean the toilets. He hopes to be ordained soon, and he said to me that it was a great reminder that all his future service was to be built on a loving willingness to serve the Lord. I think of one verger in a church in which I worked who served the Lord behind the scenes selflessly and made it possible for me to concentrate on the job I was called to do – minister the Word to people.

Thank God for such people in the life of the church.

There is a wonderful bond of love with other Christians given through regeneration. It is a grand sign of new birth into the family of God. But that love is to be worked out practically and sacrificially in our relationships one with another. That is the test of how real and genuine our love really is.

2. When are we to love?

Two events in chapter 13 form the backdrop which shows the love of Jesus in all its richness.

First, there is the betrayal of Judas. We can imagine the bombshell at the meal when Jesus said that one of them was going to betray him (13:21). It was something that brought great pain and sadness to the Saviour. In response to Peter's prompting, John asked Jesus who it was (verses 13:24, 25). Jesus replied that it was the one to whom he would give the next piece of bread.

At this point Jesus offers Judas what was probably the choice morsel given to the honoured guest at the banquet. It is a loving appeal to Judas, showing Jesus' concern about him. Indeed it has been suggested that Judas, in order to be handed this morsel privately, must have been sitting in the place of the honoured guest next to Jesus! What amazing love Jesus was showing!

John tells that when Judas had taken the bread he left 'and it was night' (13:30). In this marvellously graphic way John is telling us that there was a deeper darkness than the night outside, there was the darkness in the heart of Judas. He had been so near Jesus and yet refused to respond to his love.

The second event is the prediction of Peter's denial of Jesus (13:38). One of Jesus' closest friends would deny him when the pressure was on. One of the people that he should have been able to count on would let him down. And if outspoken Peter would do so, how concerned the rest of the disciples were becoming!

Yet it is against this backdrop that Jesus showed them his love so practically and sacrificially. So then, when are we to love? Even when it is hard to do so. Even when people let us down and betray us. Even when there is every reason not to bother, that is when we are to follow the pattern of love that Jesus gave to us.

3. Who are we to love?

Should Christians only love one another like this? Certainly Jesus has in mind that particular love that we ought to show to one another as members of the new covenant community. But of course that love is to be more spread. 'Do good to all people, especially to th belong to the family of believers' (Galatians ↑ is a particular love for members of the C⌐ but the selfless, practical love we see p is to be a mark of our lives to those (just like Jesus' love to Judas!). Even our enemies fall within the scope of this pattern of love.

He washed the feet of Judas and offered him the choice morsel, and our love too must extend beyond 'the household of faith'. We are to love our enemies like this too! What is elsewhere the teaching of the New Testament is first modelled here for us.

Verse 34 has been called the eleventh commandment! This verse has strong echoes of Ezekiel's promise of the new covenant, that will change people's hearts. Jesus has given us a reason to love, and a pattern of love to follow. We need to be obedient.

And let us not think that obedience to this command will be followed by some liturgical ceremony of footwashing. That is to miss the point. That would be to apply this passage in a wooden way. No, what we see here is a cultural expression relevant to the time, of sacrificial practical love.

What Jesus is calling us to is costly love that needs to be shown in ways that are practical today. What a challenge that is! It is not an added extra for his disciples, it is a command. It is the basis of all service for Jesus; moved by love into loving service of others for his sake. It is the mark of the disciples of Jesus *par excellence*, which shows who they follow and who has changed their lives!

4. Why are we to love?

John answers this question very vividly in his first epistle: 'We love because he first loved us' (1 John 4:19).

Jesus took the initiative in loving us even when we did not know him. His love has won our hearts, and because
have experienced the amazing quality of his love for

us, we are sensitive to his command to reflect that love to others. His love for us when we did not deserve it is the incentive to show a love in a measure like his, even when naturally we are not inclined to do so.

We love because we are joyful recipients of the love of Jesus for us. He has redeemed us, we owe him everything and so we gladly follow his commands out of love for him. The glory of our Saviour should ever be our concern, and the pattern he left for us our delight. For not only is this the way that Jesus left us to live, but it is the way of blessing and joy (13:17).

This is often not properly understood. The Lord knows what is best for us and has our interests at heart. Often his way will be hard, but we need to understand that it is the right way, the way of blessing. Sometimes young Christians feel that serving the Lord is a denial of the good things in life. How foolish that is! He is the source of life, and in following him we find life in all its fulness. It may be the way of selflessness, but then who is to say that selfishness is the secret of living! Rather, so often it is the cause of death in relationships that could otherwise have been good.

I mentioned earlier in the chapter that there are humanists who value some of the ethical teachings of Jesus, but who do not believe it possible to have a spiritual relationship with him. Yet the ethic of Christianity can never be followed without an experience of Christ's love. It i~ which is our motivation, and it is his strength i~ enables us to follow him. He provides the mo~' means. A Christless Christianity makes n~

5. What will this love achieve?

After his death and resurrection, and before he commissioned his disciples to proclaim the good news of the
Easter story, Jesus told them in the Upper Room to love
one another, and underlined this by giving a 'new commandment'. It is by this means that the world will know
who the disciples of Jesus are (13:35). By their living
after his pattern people will recognise the disciples of
Jesus. In a world full of narcissism, this pattern of love
will show a different way and point to the author of life,
Jesus himself.

In other words, the foundation of the evangelistic
mission of the church is the love the disciples of Jesus
show to one another. We will never convince non-Chris-
tians to believe in the Saviour unless they see a quality of
love in our relationships that commends our Saviour to
them. This is a very important point for every church to
grasp. No matter how good our preaching, how imagina-
tive our evangelistic events, how brilliant our music, how
attractive our premises, unless people see something of
the love of Jesus in us they will never come to believe in
him. Love for one another is the foundation of the
church's evangelistic task. I suspect it is for that reason
that some of our evangelistic strategies are unsuccessful.

6. What is in it for me?

This unworthy question is a very modern one to ask of this
passage. It is, however, a question which Jesus answers.
Too often we have swallowed the narcissist attitude of the
world of our day, and fallen for the lie that self-denial is
the way to under-achievement and unfulfilment. We have
ʼme a self-opinionated and self-absorbed society.

But Jesus tells us that those who have experienced the grace and love of God, out of gratitude to him, will seek to follow their Saviour in practical and sacrificial love; and such 'will be blessed' (13:17). There is joy and happiness in obedience to Christ's commands. His way is best, and it is the way of fulfilment. After all, he is our Maker and knows what is best for us. His way of love is not only the best way for society, but is also the way to personal self-fulfilment. So let us not be fooled by the many spurious 'life-fulfilment' alternatives! For the believer the way of joy is the way of Christ.

Let me end this chapter with relevant quotes from three of my favourite authors.

J. C. Ryle wrote: 'Knowledge without practice does not raise us above the level of the Devil.'[1] So often we tend to think that growing as a Christian means gaining more knowledge. Yes, we do need to learn more of God's ways and his commands from Scripture. But Christian growth is not about packing our heads with information; it is, rather, learning as disciples at the feet of Christ and putting what we learn into practice. It is the doing, not just the knowing of God's commands that Jesus promised would bring blessing (13:17). So let us not just believe the truth in our heads, but put it into practice in our lives. Satan knows the truth better than we, but he refuses to obey it!

'Knowledge is not entitled to be called true, unless it produces such an effect on believers as to lead them to conform themselves to their Head.'[2] So wrote John Calvin

---

1. J. C. Ryle, *Expository Thoughts on the Gospel of John*.
2. John Calvin, *Commentary on John*.

in his commentary on the Gospel of John. Real knowl-edge in a biblical sense is life-changing and Christ-honouring. Calvin puts it very well and succinctly.

Martin Luther wonderfully put the matter thus: 'Christ never gave any other commandment than that of love, because he intended that this commandment be the test of his disciples, and of true believers. For if good works and love do not blossom forth, it is not genuine faith, the gospel has not yet gained a foothold, and Christ is not yet rightly known.' Loving one another then, out of gratitude to Christ, because we have experienced the love of God for us, is the best test of how genuine our faith really is. Having benefited so by his love, we are given a marvel-lous example to follow.

In other words, Christianity is, first and foremost, not duty but joy. It is the joy of knowing and receiving the grace and love of God in Christ. It is on that basis we are called to pattern our lives on the Saviour who loves us so. The motive for so doing is not duty but gratitude. We are called to follow Christ, not in a form of drudgery or stiff-upper-lip, not in pulling our own socks up to follow the ethic of Christianity, but to follow Christ out of gratitude to him, and with his help.

'If Jesus Christ be God and died for me,' wrote the great cricketer C. T. Studd, 'then no sacrifice can be too great for me to make for him.'

Christianity is not dull, it is delightful. Don't look at the 'ianity' of Christianity, look at the Christ! It is not an ethic first of all, it is a life-changing relationship.

Chapter 3

A perspective to remember
(John 13:18-30)

There are some Christians who are kept from the service of the Lord in which they ought to be involved, simply because they have become so battered by the pressures of life and so preoccupied with their own problems. What they need is a proper perspective.

There was growing consternation and confusion in the air in the Upper Room. What the disciples thought would be a pleasant celebration meal became overshadowed with betrayal. Dark clouds gathered as Jesus encouraged them to face reality. The fact that there was betrayal amongst the disciples themselves filled them with alarm.

Judas refused the one who is the Light of the world, and the night in his own soul is mirrored by the darkness he goes out into when he leaves (13:30). John tells us that Judas had a choice. True he was prompted by Satan, but he had a choice to refuse (13:2). But that prompting, given in to and unresisted, led to the hardening of his heart. That is always what the Bible means by the 'hardening of hearts' – it means the stubborn refusal of the love of God, that leads to a complete hardness to the truth. The frightening result in Judas' case is spelled out for us in verse 27.

And yet throughout the meal we see the constant appealing, in love, of Jesus to Judas. We have already

'I am not referring to all of you; I know those I have chosen. But this is to fulfil the scripture: "He who shares my bread has lifted up his heel against me."

[19]'I am telling you now before it happens, so that when it does happen you will believe that I am He. [20]I tell you the truth, whoever accepts anyone I send accepts me; and whoever accepts me accepts the one who sent me.'

[21]After he had said this, Jesus was troubled in spirit and testified, 'I tell you the truth, one of you is going to betray me.'

[22]His disciples stared at one another, at a loss to know which of them he meant. [23]One of them, the disciple whom Jesus loved, was reclining next to him. [24]Simon Peter motioned to this disciple and said, 'Ask him which one he means.' [25]Leaning back against Jesus, he asked him, 'Lord, who is it?'

[26]Jesus answered, 'It is the one to whom I will give this piece of bread when I have dipped it in the dish.' Then, dipping the piece of bread, he gave it to Judas Iscariot, son of Simon. [27]As soon as Judas took the bread, Satan entered into him.

'What you are about to do, do quickly,' Jesus told him, [28]but no-one at the meal understood why Jesus said this to him. [29]Since Judas had charge of the money, some thought Jesus was telling him to buy what was needed for the Feast, or to give something to the poor. [30]As soon as Judas had taken the bread, he went out. And it was night (John 13:18-30).

suggested that Judas was sitting close to Jesus, quite possibly right next to him. He could have been in the place of honour when Jesus offered him the choice morsel as a final appeal of love. Peter was clearly further away from Jesus, on the other side of John, the beloved disciple (13:24).

In working on this passage I was moved as I discovered that a number of commentators think that Judas might well have had his feet washed first. This is certainly consistent with the geography of the table, which would have been long and low, with the disciples reclining either side of Jesus.

What we are seeing here is a marvellous appeal of love. Jesus was not unaware of what was going to happen to him, and he knew who would betray him. Even so he appealed in love to Judas.

John emphasises that Jesus knew all that lay ahead of him: 'Jesus knew that the time had come for him to leave this world and go to the Father' (13:1). 'Jesus knew that the Father had put all things under his power, and that he had come from God and was returning to God' (verse 3). When Jesus said, 'And you are clean, though not every one of you', John adds, lest we miss the point, 'For he knew who would betray him, and that was why he said not every one was clean' (verse 11).

To spell out the betrayal Jesus used a very picturesque description. Like a horse that raises up its hoof and 'opens' the bottom of its hoof to kick, one of the inner circle of Jesus' friends was going to kick him hard and in a way that hurt (verse 18). Spelling this out further, he talked openly of betrayal (verse 21).

Imagine the consternation! As the betrayal of Judas

became clear, not only would the disciples have felt horrified that one of their number should betray their Master, but they must have felt a personal sense of betrayal too. But in all this, Jesus was giving the disciples a perspective.

As they faced the betrayal of Judas, the denial of Peter, and the hard events that were ahead of them, Jesus took the trouble to help them see things in perspective. He wanted them to know that, as they faced the agony of betrayal and the disappointment of denial, including their corporate denial later when they all 'forsook him and fled', he knew all that lay ahead for him.

He knew that death faced him (12:32-33), and what kind of death it would be. He knew about the betrayal, their denial, his agony; yet he showed them his love, prefigured in the Upper Room by the foot-washing, and supremely displayed on the Cross. Nothing would hold him back from fulfilling the purpose for which he came. He knew his destiny and he was steadfast in fulfilling it.

It is important to remember that the death of Jesus was not the tragic end to a good man's life, a victim of circumstances, as it was portrayed in the musical *Jesus Christ Superstar*. Not a bit of it! Jesus came to die, and his death was the time of his glory! That death, however, would be very costly, and so would all the events leading up to it.

Jesus knew how terrifying the Cross would be, because for a moment the relationship between the Father and the Son would be broken, as 'he who knew no sin became sin for us' when he gave his life in our place. The horror of it, as well as the heartache of betrayal, troubled him deeply (13:21). How much Jesus went through for us!

Jesus wanted the disciples to realise that even though he knew what lay ahead, these things were not outside his control (13:3). Despite the agony and the betrayal he was still in charge, and God's purposes were being worked out. The shock of the betrayal by one of the inner circle was not to faze the disciples, because it did not faze Jesus! He expected it! He took the time and the trouble, despite what he was facing, to help the disciples come to terms with betrayal and denial in their midst.

No-one puts this point better than Calvin:

> 'And indeed, it has usually happened in the Church in almost every age, that it has had no enemies more inveterate than the members of the Church: and therefore, that believers may not have their minds disturbed by such atrocious wickedness, let them accustom themselves early to endure the attacks of traitors.'[1]

Shocks and discouragements there will be, hard and difficult times will have to be endured, but the Lord is still in control!

Furthermore, Jesus wanted them to realise who he really was. When they would see the things come to pass that he had carefully told them of, they would know who he really was. There is a clear claim to deity in verse 19: 'I am telling you now before it happens, so that when it does happen you will believe that I am He.' The Greek phrase translated 'I am He' is used in the Septuagint rendering of Isaiah 43:10 in reference to Yahweh. Despite all the trauma of these days, their faith would be strengthened when they began to understand who Jesus really was

---

1. John Calvin, *Commentary on John*.

and what he came to do, and how he had fulfilled God's wonderful plan of redemption.

This perspective which Jesus taught the disciples needs to be grasped by us. Despite their failures and folly Jesus loved his disciples still. A first look at verse 20 makes one wonder why it is there: 'I tell you the truth, whoever accepts anyone I send accepts me; and whoever accepts me accepts the one who sent me.' It seems strangely jarring and appears, at first, unconnected with the previous verse.

But the connection is grand and wonderful. In spite of betrayal in the midst of the professing church, in spite of their own failures and sins, Jesus loved those he had chosen, and he had a job for them to do.

We may be tempted to give up on ourselves at times, but he never gives up on us, and has a purpose for us to fulfil with his authority. Like Peter, we will sometimes find denial in our own hearts, and maybe even see betrayal of Jesus by those we thought were disciples. But the Lord never gives up on his real followers.

Sometimes in the professing church we will find leaders who betray the Lord and his Word. Sad and tragic as that is, and grieving as it is to the heart of the Lord, it should not throw us, any more than it threw our Master. He is still in control. He hasn't 'lost it' because there is disappointment with some leaders.

In the church there will be real heartaches and disappointments. I was talking to someone recently who is a fine Christian. The person said to me: 'I have been so hurt by some Christians that I cannot bring myself to go to church again.' It happens and it is tragic, but it is folly to allow ourselves to be defeated by it. As in the case of my friend, there is the real danger of hurt becoming a sin that keeps us away from the involvement and fellowship that we need. Sometimes real believers, like Peter, will hurt us and disappoint us deeply, and no doubt we will disappoint them too; but the Lord, who doesn't give up on us, calls us not to give up on one another.

The church in Britain today is not, despite many encouragements, going through its best period of history. There is denial of the truths of the written Word of God which describe the living Word of God, our Saviour. Sad as that is, and resisted as it must be, it should not throw us.

Also, even amongst some real Christians, there will be deep hurt and pain. Let us learn to forgive as we, in love, have been forgiven. Maybe you feel disappointed, even hurt right now by the fellowship to which you belong, and it is hindering your love and service for Christ. We need to learn to recognise Peter in all of us, and learn to love one another with a practical love which is not easily put off, for that is the kind of love Jesus showed to the disciples.

Let us keep our eyes on him, our sovereign Lord, and, in doing so, keep a right perspective on life. Generally life will bring its fair share of heartaches and heartbreak to the Christian, as well as to everyone else. Hard times can debilitate, but in them Jesus invites us to see that he knows, cares and can be trusted to work things out to his glory and for our good.

We need not be thrown by disappointment or suffering, rather we should remind ourselves that the Lord who loved us, and died for us, is still the sovereign Lord. If we belong to him, he has a purpose for us to fulfil. May his love fill us, encourage us, and motivate us to loving service for him.

SECTION 2

The Last Question Time

Chapter 4

Asking questions

In the west of Ireland, people are famous for not answering directly questions that are put to them. Instead they answer a question with another question.

The story is told about two American visitors to Connemara who had been warned about this and had indeed noticed that whenever they asked a question, they were asked another question by way of reply. So one morning the husband determined to break through this and get a straight answer. He went into the local village, to the Post Office. There was a local wag sitting on the window-sill, and the American said to him, 'Is this the Post Office?' And the local answered: 'Would it be stamps you are looking for?'!

When we come to look at the end of John chapter 13 and through chapter 14, we see that after Judas left, the conversation Jesus had with the disciples revolved around four questions.

Remember that the disciples are troubled in heart. There is growing consternation among them because of the threat from the Pharisees and the leaders of the Jews, the prediction of Jesus of the betrayal by one of his most intimate circle of friends, and the announcement of Jesus' own departure.[1] In addition the clear statement by Jesus

---

1. This whole section of discussion (13:31-14:31) is bracketed by the key point that Jesus is making to them, that he is actually leaving them (13:33; 14:28).

that Peter would disown and deny him added to their concern. No doubt the other disciples were saying something like this: 'If that's what's going to happen to outspoken, dynamic Peter, what's going to happen to the rest of us?'

But we find not only four questions *from* troubled hearts, but four answers *for* troubled hearts from the lips of the Lord Jesus himself.

Jesus had informed them in 13:31: 'Now is the Son of Man glorified and God is glorified in him. If God is glorified in him, then God will glorify the Son in himself (the 'himself' is referring to the Father, it seems to me). Jesus is saying, as it were: 'I want you to see that the glory of me, the Son of God, is wrapped up with the glory of the Father, and the glory of the Father is wrapped up with the glory of the Son.'

Then he directly addressed their developing anguish: 'Do not let your hearts be troubled' (14:1). He wanted to encourage them now that events were becoming difficult for them to appreciate. The chain of events leading to his Passion had begun with Judas' departure. It is not difficult to imagine the sadness, the consternation, the troubled hearts of these disciples. Neither is it surprising, given their consternation at what Jesus is saying to them, that questions came to their minds.

Merrill Tenney in his commentary on John's Gospel writes: 'Their uncertainty and their discouragement had weakened them and he wanted to strengthen them against complete collapse in the imminent tragedy that lay ahead.'[2] Jesus used their uncertainties, their bewilderment and

2. Merrill C. Tenney, *John*, Expositors Bible Commentary, Zondervan, 1981, p. 143.

their questions, and he addressed them directly and helped them through their problems.

Their questions did show confusion and lack of understanding. But it isn't surprising that they wanted to ask the questions that are recorded by John. Remember, on many occasions Jesus taught by questions. In the Gospel accounts, he often used questions to draw out of people a perspective on the truth, to make them think about important things.

Jesus could handle the questions from their troubled hearts, and he can handle our questions too. We need to learn that, like the disciples in the Upper Room, whatever questions come from our troubled hearts at times, Jesus can handle them. As he did there, he can use our questions as an opportunity to teach and help us grow in understanding.

As we bring questions from our troubled hearts to Jesus and to the light of his Word of truth, we will find a way through. We may not find the answer which we expect. We may not be told all that we wish to know this side of glory, but we will be given enough to see us through the challenge or the difficulty that may be troubling us.

In the next four chapters, we will look at these four questions recorded in this passage of John's Gospel.

Chapter 5

'Lord, where are you going?'
(John 13:31-14:4)

Simon Peter asked Jesus, 'Lord, where are you going?'
Jesus replied, 'Where I am going you cannot follow now,
but you will follow later.'

Peter's question was a response to what Jesus had said
in verse 33: 'My children, I will be with you only a little
longer. You will look for me, and just as I told the Jews,
so I tell you now. Where I am going you cannot come.'
Peter's reply shows that he did not understand the reference of Jesus to his departure, although judging by verse
37, Peter had some idea that death is threatening the one
whom he has followed and whom he loves.

Let us think about Peter. Generally, it is helpful to look
at characters in the Bible for they show us the kind of
people that are among the disciples of Jesus, the people
whom he loves and doesn't give up on despite their
frailties and foibles.

Firstly, consider the *confused devotion* of Peter. His
affection for Jesus, though often expressed clumsily, was
undeniably genuine. He really loved the Lord Jesus. As
Don Carson writes about him: 'Knowledge of the Master's plans and continued intimacy with him are more
attractive than obedience.'[1] He wanted to be with Jesus;
he wanted that developing closeness with Jesus. That was

---

1. D. A. Carson, *The Gospel According to John*, IVP, 1991, p. 486.

When he was gone, Jesus said, 'Now is the Son of Man glorified and God is glorified in him. [32]If God is glorified in him, God will glorify the Son in himself, and will glorify him at once.

[33]'My children, I will be with you only a little longer. You will look for me, and just as I told the Jews, so I tell you now: Where I am going, you cannot come.

[34]'A new command I give you: Love one another. As I have loved you, so you must love one another. [35]By this all men will know that you are my disciples, if you love one another.'

[36]Simon Peter asked him, 'Lord, where are you going?'

Jesus replied, 'Where I am going, you cannot follow now, but you will follow later.'

[37]Peter asked, 'Lord, why can't I follow you now? I will lay down my life for you.'

[38]Then Jesus answered, 'Will you really lay down your life for me? I tell you the truth, before the cock crows, you will disown me three times!

[1]'Do not let your hearts be troubled. Trust in God; trust also in me. [2]In my Father's house are many rooms; if it were not so, I would have told you. I am going there to prepare a place for you. [3]And if I go and prepare a place for you, I will come back and take you to be with me that you also may be where I am. [4]You know the way to the place where I am going' (John 13:31-14:4).

more attractive to him than obedience to what Jesus was commanding at this point in time.

Secondly, Peter showed *characteristic oscillation*. Remember the conversation between Jesus and Peter earlier in the chapter, where Peter says to Jesus, 'Are you going to wash my feet?' (13:6). 'Don't do that!' says Peter. Then Jesus says: 'Unless I wash you, you have no part with me' (13:8). And then Peter swung from refusal to accept Jesus' ways, to saying: 'Well, if you are going to wash me, don't just wash my feet, but wash me totally.' We find, at the end of the chapter, the same kind of oscillation in Peter.

Peter was the kind of person who does not have an even temperament; rather he was the type who have great 'highs' and perhaps considerable 'lows'. Look at his oscillating in verses 37 and 38: between, on the one hand, martyrdom, his willingness to lay down his life for Jesus; and on the other hand, Jesus making Peter face what he was really like, that he was actually going to disown Jesus.

Thirdly, there was in Peter *a greater desire than he had the capacity to fulfil*. Again, let me quote Carson: 'Sadly, good intentions in a secure room, after good food, are far less attractive in a darkened garden, with a hostile mob. At this point in his pilgrimage, Peter's intentions and self-assessment vastly outstrip his strength.'[2]

It is true, isn't it, that we too, in the context of Christian worship with all its joy, in the delight of a situation like a convention or houseparty, can promise the Lord everything. But it is when we are back at work or back in a difficult family situation, that our love and our obedience are really tested. That is the real crunch of how serious we

---

2. D. A. Carson, *The Gospel According to John*, IVP, 1991, p. 486.

are in our commitment to Jesus. It is true that our desire to serve God can sometimes outstrip our gifting and our ability and, indeed, our maturity to serve him.

I can remember once going to sit an exam when I was a student in Bristol. There were six of us piled in a car, going to the very last exam that I took at theological college. The exam was on one of my favourite subjects – Reformation Church history. When we opened the exam paper, we all got a shock. It was everything that we had not swotted up! What our tutor had told us, and what we had worked out was going to be asked, didn't appear! We just had to make the best of it that we could.

I remember the return journey, with nearly all of us feeling the same – dejected! But there's always one, isn't there! There was one who said: 'Hallelujah! Isn't it wonderful! That's the best paper I've had in ages!' The rest of us said, 'We are happy for you, but shut up, brother!' But when the results arrived, he was the only one who failed; the rest of us, in God's mercy, passed. Sad for him! Sometimes our enthusiasm outstrips our maturity, doesn't it? That was the case with Peter.

Fourthly, there was also a *characteristic impatience* in Peter: 'Lord, why can't I follow you now?' (13:37). He wanted to get on immediately with what he thought was the way to go. Look at how Jesus answered him (14:1).

At this point I would like to remind you that the chapter divisions are not always helpful! They are not in the original text, but were put in later, so that we could find our way around! Here the chapter division is very unhelpful.

In 14:1 Jesus is still talking to Peter, although he has broadened it out to all the disciples, because Peter was so often the spokesman for what they all felt. Jesus is saying to all of them: 'Don't let your hearts be troubled!' But if he is saying that to all of them, he is saying it as a direct answer to Peter's question.

What did Peter need to understand at this point? He, and the others, needed to trust God. Verse 1 may read: 'You trust in God; you trust in me', or it may read: 'You trust in God', then the imperative: 'Trust in me.' I think it is preferable to take both in the imperative: 'Trust in God, Peter, and trust in me also.'

What a remarkable combination! Against a background of Jewish theology, it is remarkable that Jesus puts those two imperatives together: 'Trust in God and trust just as much in me.' Unless Jesus was the unique Son of God and equal with the Father, how could he encourage such an attitude?

Jesus was saying, 'Peter, if you are to get through the bewilderment of life, if you are to have a settlement to your troubled heart (and the others to have that too), I want you to understand that you must have a heavenly perspective on your earthly pilgrimage.' Isn't it interesting that the first response of Jesus to troubled hearts in the Upper Room is to talk to them about heaven?

We, too, need to have a perspective on heaven if we are to get through the challenges and the problems of Christian living here on earth.

It is very interesting how Jesus focuses on heaven. Look at what he says about it in these verses.

1. Heaven is a real place

I always get upset when I see heaven portrayed as a place where people float around on clouds, in ephemeral garments, as if the whole experience is not real. As an

Irishman the only thing I like about that portrayal is the harps! But these are vague pictures of heaven. Jesus says: 'No, that is not the way it is, heaven is a real place, it is my Father's house.'

The world in which we live has a pull upon us. It is difficult in our generation, which is very concerned with the immediate and now, to focus on the heavenly reality. But as disciples of Jesus, if our hearts are to be settled in the context of the troubles that come to us and test our faith, then we must have a heavenly perspective on things.

Jesus says, 'Here is a house, here is a home, here is a reality, here is a place I am familiar with, for it is my Father's house.' But Jesus says there is more: 'In my Father's house are many rooms' (14:2). What a meal some commentators and preachers have made of this phrase, 'In my Father's house are many rooms.'

I was once at a conference where somebody said, 'Jesus said that in heaven there are many rooms. There is a place for Christians, there is a place for Moslems, there is a place for good-hearted, ethically-minded humanists.' I couldn't believe it! It was so contrary to what Jesus said in this passage. It was an absurd instance of taking a verse out of context and misunderstanding and misusing it.

So what does Jesus mean by saying that his Father's house has many rooms? He is saying to the disciples who are troubled, who are wondering what the future holds for them: 'Look, I want to tell you that your future is heaven. Your future is with me in my Father's house. I want you to know there is room for all of you. Peter, I have just told you that you are going to disown me; but there is room for you. The rest of you, troubled and distressed, confused and bewildered, there is room for you too, for in my Father's house are many rooms.'

'If it were not so, I would have told you' (14:2). 'If I wasn't going back to the Father, with whom I spent eternity before, would I not have told you? Would I not have told you that there wasn't enough room for you? I am going there to prepare a place for you to come too.'

Heaven is a real place.

2. Heaven is a prepared place

'I am going there to prepare a place for you' (14:2c).

This is a promise, not to all and sundry, but to the disciples of Jesus, and exclusively to them. Nobody drifts into heaven. Heaven is a prepared place for those who have become disciples of Jesus.

I love the story of the old Scottish crofter, who lived in the Highlands. His minister came to visit him after a particularly bad storm. The minister said: 'I have come to see you as I was worried in case, in the severity of the storm, your thatched roof had blown off.' The crofter replied: 'I did not wait until the storm, Minister, to thatch my roof. I thatched it securely before the storm came!' He had made wise preparation before it was too late.

God, in his mercy, offers the possibility of sharing eternity with him. If we prepare by faith in Jesus for meeting our Maker after we die, then we are ready. Heaven is a prepared place for prepared people.

But look at verse 2, a verse that has blessed me personally. I thought, at one time, that the verse was saying that Jesus was going to prepare a place, and that, somehow, after his Resurrection and Ascension, Jesus was getting heaven ready for the arrival of all his disciples.

But that's not what Jesus was saying at all. As if heaven needed the rearrangement of the curtains, and the constant spring-cleaning of the rooms, so that they might be ready for the arrival of the disciples!

Jesus was saying that it was his going from the disciples that prepared for them a place in heaven. Isn't that glorious? It is the death, it is the departure of Jesus, it is the suffering and pain of Jesus, it is the cross of Jesus, that prepares a place for the disciples in heaven.

Bishop J. C. Ryle commented: 'Heaven is a holy place. Its inhabitants are holy. To be happy in heaven, it stands to reason we must be prepared for it. Our hearts must be somewhat in tune, somewhat ready for it.' [3]

Heaven, the real place, is a prepared place for prepared people.

3. Heaven is a meeting place

Jesus said: 'If I go and prepare a place for you, I will come back and take you to be with me that you also may be where I am' (verse 3).

Isn't that tremendous? What is at the heart of our questions about heaven? Is it not, What will it be like? The answer is, It is where Jesus is; it is where the disciples of Jesus will be. What a glorious picture of heaven that is! Isn't that all we need to know about heaven? It is where our Saviour is, where we will see him face to face, and where all the disciples for whom he has opened heaven will be with him.

What a glorious meeting that will be! How wonderful it will be to see our Saviour face to face whom we have trusted by faith! How wonderful to be in the presence of

---

3. J C Ryle, *Expository Thoughts on the Gospels*.

all those who have come to know, follow and love Jesus, who for the first time in all eternity are together! How good to see loved ones who have gone before!

I like very much the comment of Joni Eareckson Tada: 'Of all the things that will surprise us when we see Christ face to face, this, I believe, will surprise us most: that we did not love Christ more before we died.'[4]

As we stand back and think about Jesus' answer to Peter's question we see that *Peter needed to understand the uniqueness of the sacrificial death of Jesus*.

Jesus said to Peter: 'You cannot come now' (13:36). 'You cannot follow me now, Peter, because you cannot take part in what I am doing for you. Nobody can take part in my unique sacrificial sin-bearing work on the cross. It is only me, the righteous for the unrighteous, who can do that. It is only me as perfect Man, and fully God, that can die as the Mediator to bring God and man together. But you can follow me later. Because of what I have done, you can come later to my Father's house, which my going has prepared for you and for all my disciples.'

Later, Peter would look back and understand this. He could not follow then, but he would ultimately. He, and the other disciples, needed a grip on heaven if they were to set their troubled hearts at rest.

I repeat, we need to keep our minds on heaven. We have no abiding city here. We are resident aliens in this world. We do not belong here; our home is our Father's house in heaven. That is where we really belong; that's where we are going to; that is our destiny, and unless we keep our eyes fixed on that, we will lose the right

---

4. Joni Eareckson Tada, *Diamonds In The Dust*, Zondervan, 1993 (the reading for May 7).

perspective on the troubles of life.

This side of glory there are injustices, there are difficult problems that we have to face. This side of glory there are sometimes questions that we don't have clear answers to and, unless we keep our eyes on what Jesus came to do, we will become over-troubled.

In the previous church that I worked in, one of my churchwardens/fellow elders had been to farming college. One day on a church outing, as we were walking over one of the very few hills on the Cheshire plain, we looked over that attractive county. It was just the time of the year when the farmers had been doing a lot of ploughing.

Looking down on these huge fields with row upon row of furrows, I said to my friend, Roy: 'It's amazing! How on earth did the farmer plough such straight furrows? Looking down on that field, it's almost as if he has drawn a line across it with a ruler.'

Roy replied, 'It's really quite easy. What you do is that you sit in your tractor at one side of the field and fix your eyes on a point in the hedge on the other side. As you drive along you never take your eye off the point in the hedge on the other side. And if you do that you plough a straight furrow. Once you take your eye off that point, once you take your eye off the destination you are heading towards, then you get a wobble in the furrow.'

What a good illustration of our need to keep our eyes on heaven, in order to keep a heavenly perspective. That is where Jesus begins in answering the questions of troubled hearts. They needed to trust him and keep their eyes on their destination, and so do we.

Chapter 6

'How can we know the way?'
(John 14:5, 6)

When I visited Hampton Court I was really impressed by its famous maze. I have always been fascinated by mazes. Inside, there are long, straight paths that seem to be leading in the right direction; but then suddenly there is a bend, and then another, so that one is taken completely by surprise. It is all too easy to lose one's way. I can remember one or two moments at Hampton Court when the feeling that I would never get out made me start to panic!

Many people's lives are rather like travelling through a maze. There are the pleasant and exciting times when all seems to be going right. Some just live for those pleasant times, such as the birth of a baby, a rise in salary, a continental summer holiday, or a new car. But the unexpected turns and twists of life must be faced too!

Many people live with no real sense of direction through life, and no real hope of anything beyond it. Deep down, if they stopped to admit it, they feel lost. They do not give much thought to this life or to life beyond this maze.

Others know that they need religious answers to the deep questions about life, but they reason something like this: 'What is really important is sincerity. If we are sincere in what we believe, we will get there in the end.

All roads that are followed in sincerity lead to God.'
However, if such would examine the great faiths of the
world they would see that each of these faiths has a very
different view of God and the way to a relationship with
him.

Some faiths see God as not to be known apart from in
creation. They understand God to be so involved with it
as to be virtually indistinguishable from created things.
But the Christian view is of a personal God who made the
world and sustains it by his power, and who stepped into
human history in the person of his unique Son, Jesus
Christ, in order to redeem a people to whom to show his
amazing love. The Christian view is further removed
from other religions than Tokyo is from New York. All
roads that lead even to Tokyo or New York are not
demonstrably going in the same direction!

Jesus' answer to Thomas' question has deep relevance
to the views stated above. Before we can see that fully, we
must understand something of Thomas' character, and
also examine carefully Jesus' answer to his question.

We do not know much about Thomas, and most of
what we can know is found in John's Gospel. Let us look
at three passages which give us a clear insight into the
kind of person Thomas was.

> Thomas said to him, 'Lord, we don't know where
> you are going, so how can we know the way?'
>   Jesus answered, 'I am the way and the truth and
> the life. No-one comes to the Father except through
> me' (John 14:5, 6).

1. A sceptical person (John 20:24-28)

In this most well-known passage about Thomas, he was absent from the disciples when Jesus first appeared to them after the resurrection. When they told Thomas that they had seen the Lord, he was sceptical: 'Unless I see the nail marks in his hands and put my finger where the nails were, and put my hand into his side, I will not believe it' (20:25).

Thomas had a somewhat sceptical disposition, he wasn't one to be convinced easily! He needed real evidence to believe what none of the disciples had expected would happen. Yet he is convinced by the appearance of Jesus, and from his lips comes one of the most forthright statements of faith in Jesus in the whole of the New Testament: 'My Lord and my God' (20:28).

'Only the plainest of evidence could have convinced a sceptic like Thomas. But convinced he was, which shows us the evidence was incontrovertible.'[1] So Thomas was something of a sceptic.

2. A confused and perplexed person (John 14:5f.)

In this passage the occasion for Thomas asking his question is the comment of Jesus in the previous verse: 'You know the way to the place where I am going.' Thomas replied that he is not at all clear what Jesus is talking about – what does he mean by 'the Father's house' and how would the disciples get there?

Here is a confused and perplexed disciple. As Merrill Tenney puts it: 'His question reveals a man who was confused by life, and felt its riddles were insolvable' though 'not ready to accept a state of permanent bewilder-

---

1. Leon Morris, *John*, Marshall, Morgan and Scott, 1972, p. 851.

ment'. [2] He wanted an answer. He is a disciple with deep confusion and questions.

3. A melancholic person (John 11:16)
This reference is not so well-known, but it is instructive in building a portrait of Thomas.

Jesus had just been told the news that Lazarus had died. He knew that God had a purpose to strengthen the disciples' faith as they would see what their Master was to do. So Jesus told them: 'Let us go to him' (11:15). Thomas' reply is interesting: 'Let us also go, that we may die with him.'

There is realism there, for Jerusalem was becoming a dangerous place for Jesus and the disciples. However, there is also courage and loyalty expressed to Jesus – despite the danger, Thomas will go.

But there is also *a streak of sarcastic melancholy* in Thomas, as if he was thinking, 'OK, we'll go with Jesus if he wants that madness, but we will probably die with him there!' That was over-pessimistic and showed an inclination to look on the dark side.

Have you some people in your church family who love to be miserable, who have a tendency to look on the glum side? When I was a young curate on Merseyside, working in the church in which I began my ordained ministry, I remember a graphic illustration of this point. We had two churchwardens, one optimistic by nature, the other inclined to be sometimes pessimistic. The church was growing, and one morning before a service, one warden came in and said to my vicar, 'Praise the Lord, the church

2. Merrill C. Tenney, *John*, Expositors Bible Commentary, Zondervan, 1981, p. 144.

is half-full this morning.' Shortly afterwards the other warden came in and said, 'The church is half-empty this morning!'

I think that Thomas was a bit like the second warden! Here is a 'loyal, even courageous disciple, but one who is liberally endowed with misapprehensions and doubts.' [3] He is 'honest, pessimistic and uninhibited'.[4] He has a tendency to see the dark side in all its starkness! I know people like that, and I'm sure you do too! But thank God for Thomas' honesty and his willingness to be convinced, because he called forth a brilliant answer from Jesus.

The answer of Jesus to perplexity and confusion is not a recipe, but a relationship. Let us consider the magnificent reply of Jesus.

Jesus answered, 'I am the way and the truth and the life. No-one comes to the Father except through me' (14:6). Of the three statements in the first sentence of the verse, the one that is emphasised is the first: 'I am the way'; for this is what relates directly to Thomas' question in verse 5: 'How can we know the way?'

Please notice carefully the connection between the first and the last part of verse 6. Jesus is *the* way because he is the *only* way to the Father. In this generation, with a good intentioned naivety and foolishness, many like to think that contradictory things, if sincerely held, will be all right in the end.

We live in a fuzzy-headed age with little concern for the truth. But God is there, a truth people know instinctively in their hearts though they try to suppress it; and if

---

3. D. A. Carson, *The Gospel According to John*, IVP, 1991 p. 490.
4. Merrill C. Tenney, *John*, Expositors Bible Commentary, Zondervan, 1981, p. 144.

he has revealed in his Son, Jesus Christ, the way to a personal relationship with him, then that closes down all the alternative ways to God that people might wish to follow. It closes them down because he does not approve of them, because they are blind alleys which lead nowhere but to ruin.

God has revealed the only way to a relationship with himself, and that is through his Son. This has sometimes been called 'the scandal of particularity' in Christianity.

How is Jesus the only way to God and his heaven? Because Jesus is 'the truth'. At the beginning of his Gospel John wrote: 'No-one has ever seen God, but God the only Son, who is at the Father's side, has made him known' (John 1:18). Jesus is the one who tells us the truth about God and shows us what he is like. Jesus is the one who tells us the truth about the world, why humans are here, and the purpose for which they were made. Jesus is the one that comes as the Light of the world to shine into people's lives and show them the truth about themselves, that they are sinners in need of God's mercy and forgiveness.

In short there is no real truth about God, the world, or ourselves, apart from Jesus, for he is the truth. People may look for answers elsewhere and think they have found some, but they are not true, rather they are lies. Jesus is the way to God because he is the truth. Apart from Jesus no crucial truth can be known.

John also wrote that 'In him was life, and the life was the light of men' (John 1:4). Jesus is the way to God and the way to heaven because there is no life apart from him. He has given life, the very breath people breathe is given to them by him. Jesus was God's agent in creation and he continually sustains it. There can be no natural life apart from him, and there can be no eternal life without being in relationship with him by faith. 'Jesus is the way to God precisely because he is the truth of God and the life of God ... He so mediated God's truth and God's life that he is the very way to God.' [5]

Notice what Jesus doesn't say. He doesn't say that he *knows* the way, but rather he *is* the way. Jesus' answer to the perplexity and confusion that Thomas finds in life, is a personal relationship with himself. In a very real sense, his answer to Thomas is the same as the answer to Peter earlier, 'Trust me and follow me.' It is interesting that the early Christians were called 'followers of the Way' before they were called 'Christians', which actually is a nickname.

Nor does Jesus say that he is *a* way, a means of knowing truth, and a means of discovering what life is all about. It is not that Jesus is one of a number of alternatives. It is not that he is the best of the alternatives either. He is *the* way, because no-one can know the Father and be in his heaven except by coming first to his Son. That is the truth of it.

To the uncertain, perplexed and doubtful about life and life's problems – Jesus is the way. Stick to him, and trust in him. Think back to the picture of the maze – Jesus is the way through life to God's heaven. How foolish we are if we do not follow him!

5. D. A. Carson, *The Gospel According to John*, IVP, 1991 p. 491.

Chapter 7

'Lord, show us the Father'
(John 14:7-14)

Philip said, 'Lord, show us the Father, and that will be enough for us' (14:8). You might say: 'That isn't a question.' Well, actually it is. The very real question underlying the words is this: How can I experience God? How can I see God? How can I know God?

Let's just think for a moment of the kind of person that Philip was. There is misunderstanding and confusion in Philip's heart, just as there was in Thomas' heart. To quote Merrill Tenney: 'If Thomas was a sceptic, Philip was a realist.'[1] And Tenney, although I think he overstates his case, goes on to say: 'Philip was materialistic. Apparently abstractions meant little to him. Nevertheless he had a deep desire to experience God for himself.' Philip certainly had a deep desire to experience God, and yes, he was impatient with abstractions, but I think it is too much to say he was materialistic.

Philip wanted a real answer. He was the type of person who wanted to 'cut to the chase', who wanted to get to the end of the story; the sort of person who picks up a detective story and reads the last bit before they read what is in the middle! He was the kind of person who wants to

---

1. Merrill C. Tenney, *John*, Expositors Bible Commentary, Zondervan, 1981, p. 145.

'... If you really knew me, you would know my Father as well. From now on, you do know him and have seen him.'

[8]Philip said, 'Lord, show us the Father and that will be enough for us.'

[9]Jesus answered: 'Don't you know me, Philip, even after I have been among you such a long time? Anyone who has seen me has seen the Father. How can you say, "Show us the Father"? [10]Don't you believe that I am in the Father, and that the Father is in me? The words I say to you are not just my own. Rather, it is the Father, living in me, who is doing his work. [11]Believe me when I say that I am in the Father and the Father is in me; or at least believe on the evidence of the miracles themselves. [12]I tell you the truth, anyone who has faith in me will do what I have been doing. He will do even greater things than these, because I am going to the Father. [13]And I will do whatever you ask in my name, so that the Son may bring glory to the Father. [14]You may ask me for anything in my name, and I will do it ...' (John 14:7-14).

be practical and get down to the nitty-gritty. I wonder if you are like him?

This answer Jesus gave is the only one of the four answers that is tinged with a degree of sadness. There are three aspects to the answer:

First, 'Don't you know me, Philip, even after I have been among you such a long time?' (verse 9).

Philip did not seem to understand that Jesus was the one who perfectly revealed the Father. As the incarnate Son of God, Jesus, to quote Don Carson, 'narrates God'.[2] As John himself wrote earlier in his Gospel: 'No-one has ever seen God, but God the only Son, who is at the Father's side, has made him known' (1:18). Jesus was saying to Philip, 'Don't you understand that I have revealed to you God himself? As the eternal Son of God I am God, and when you see me, you see God.'

Secondly, Jesus speaks about the closeness of his relationship with his Father, and makes a clear claim to deity: 'He that has seen me has seen the Father.'

Let me again quote Don Carson: 'No mere envoy would refer to the one who sent him as his Father, claim that whoever has seen him had seen the Father, and affirm mutual indwelling between himself and the one who sent him.'[3] No godly man would do that no matter how special, no matter how unique.

Thirdly, Jesus is revealing that he and the Father are one, in a unique relationship, and as the unique Son of God he reveals the Father. He is the One through whom alone the Father is known. If Philip wanted to know God

2. D. A. Carson, *The Gospel According to John*, IVP, 1991 p. 491.
3. *ibid*, p. 494, 495.

and experience him, then he needed to have a relationship with Jesus.

These aspects are of tremendous importance in a pluralistic society, as inter-faith dialogue becomes an issue faced by many churches.

I was at a meeting recently and afterwards said to another minister: 'What are you doing in your church about the decade of evangelism?' He replied: 'I am very embarrassed about the decade of evangelism. We are doing nothing.' I asked: 'Why is that?' And he replied: 'Because I believe that all roads lead to God, and Jesus is just one way.' I then said to him: 'Do you believe that Jesus is the best way, the most special way to God?' (though I would want to say more than that). He said: 'No, I wouldn't even say that. He is simply the cultural way to God that I have accepted and he stands on a level plain with all others.'

I couldn't resist saying to him: 'How do you square that with the convictions of the early Christians?' He replied: 'I can't, but I won't even try either!' What a tragedy! What an appalling comment from somebody who should be a minister of the gospel of Jesus Christ! He should have been encouraging his church to live out Christ and witness to him as the only one who reveals God.

There is a lot of interest today in 'spirituality' and in getting to know 'God'. But the prevailing view of 'God' is a very vague one. What the church needs to say is that the only way that God will be experienced and known, both now and in eternity, is through Jesus. He is the only way to the Father, because in him is all the truth about God, and in him alone is the life of God.

John records important statements of Jesus in 14:11-

14 and they deserve careful consideration. Let us examine them.

First, 'If you won't believe my words, believe in me on the evidence of the miracles themselves' (14:11). What is Jesus saying? He is saying that his miracles, his works as well as his words, are signposts displaying who he actually is.

Secondly, 'I tell you the truth, anyone who has faith in me will do what I have been doing. He will do even greater things than these because I am going to the Father' (14:12). There has been a lot of confusion in evangelical circles about the meaning of this verse. Even if you disagree with my explanation, please think it through, because I believe the issue is very important.

I found myself recently on a conference platform with a fine Christian teacher whom I greatly respect. Concerning this verse he said: 'We will, in the church today, do things that Jesus could not do and the apostles did not do. But we will do them today, because this verse promises that we will do greater things; we will do more wonderful things than Jesus did.' My question to him was: 'What does that do to your doctrine of the deity of Jesus, and the uniqueness of the events of the ministry of Jesus?'

I don't think that is the way to understand verse 12, and I will tell you why I think so.

Look at John 5:20-23, to what C. H. Dodd called 'the parable of the apprentice'[4]: 'For the Father loves the Son and shows him all he does' (or 'all his trade', Dodd). 'Yet he will show him even greater things than these' (using the same phrase as John 14:12). 'For just as the Father

---

4. C. H. Dodd, *Historical Tradition in the Fourth Gospel*, Cambridge, 1963, p. 386, n. 2.

raises the dead and gives them life, even so the Son gives life to whom he is pleased to give it. Moreover, the Father judges no-one but has entrusted all judgment to the Son, that all may honour the Son just as they honour the Father.'

What is being said there is that because of the Resurrection of the Lord Jesus, he will bring life to many. He will be the judge of the world, because as the Giver of life and as the Saviour he has the right to do so, and we must therefore one day stand before him. In the context of these verses 'the greater works' is of people being brought to resurrection and eternal life.

This interpretation fits in with John 6:28-29. The question asked there is: 'What must we do to do the works God requires?' Jesus answered, 'The work of God is this: to believe in the one he has sent.' If I may put it like this, everything that God is about – his 'work' – is to bring people to a belief and a trust in his Son, because it is through that commitment and that relationship with Jesus that he is glorified, we get to know God, and we find a place in the Father's house.

In John 14:12, the 'greater things' is a reference to two things:

First, it is not greater works *in degree* – what more spectacular things could be done than the raising of Lazarus, or the stilling of the storm, or the feeding of the five thousand? – but greater works *in extent*. There will be many more converts through the missionary activity of the apostles, and the church down the ages. Instead of Jesus being, as it were, contained in one land, there will be the universal mission of the church.

Furthermore there would be greater *clarity* in the

ministry of the apostles, in what they are able to proclaim about Jesus – in the light of the events of Calvary, his resurrection and the coming of the Holy Spirit – than could be declared before, even through the ministry of Jesus himself. 'The words and deeds of Jesus were somewhat veiled during the days of his flesh.'[5] The saving events would in the future be proclaimed clearly.

So, there will be greater works in extent as more believe, and there will also be greater clarity in the evangelistic mission of the church because the events of Easter and Pentecost would have taken place.

There is one other important point here that can very easily be neglected. Jesus goes on immediately to say in verses 13 and 14: 'I will do whatever you ask in my name[6], so that the Son may bring glory to the Father. You may ask me for anything in my name, and I will do it.' Why is he saying that?

He is saying: 'Look, you are troubled, you are dispirited' (and there may be troubled and discouraged disciples reading these words now). Jesus said to the disciples, and would say to us: 'I have work for you to do. I have greater things for you to do, and the means for you to do them is to ask me, to trust me in prayer. Cast yourselves on me that I might do it through you. You will be the means of blessing to many, and you will find blessing yourself. The key to your success is prayer.'

---

5. D. A. Carson, *The Gospel According to John*, IVP, 1991, p. 496.
6. I will comment on the meaning of 'in my name' in the Chapter entitled 'Christian Joy'.

Chapter 8

'Why show yourself to us and not to the world?' (John 14:22-24)

First of all in this chapter I will look at the question Judas asked Jesus and see what lessons we can learn from Judas' outlook as well as from Jesus' answer. Then, secondly, I will include, by way of a conclusion, a short survey of what we have learned from the four questions that the disciples had asked Jesus in the Upper Room.

Judas' question is very simply: 'Why is it that you are going to reveal yourself just to the disciples, and not to the whole of the community?' (14:22).

It seems that Judas (of whom little is known) was particularly captive to the view of his time which was that the Messianic king would establish a visible kingdom, and expel the Romans. He had understood only one strand of Old Testament teaching. He thought that 'If Jesus is the Messianic king then he must startle the world with apocalyptic self-disclosure.'[1] But Jesus was saying: 'No, I am also the suffering servant' (cf. Isaiah 53). 'My kingship is not of this world, in that sense.'

Certainly at the second advent, when the Lord Jesus returns, everybody will see who he is, but not until then. But Judas was blinkered by his culture, and by his tradition, and the misunderstanding of those in the professing church of his day who didn't see fully what the Old

---

1. D. A. Carson, *The Gospel According to John*, IVP, 1991, p. 504.

Testament prophets had foretold about the coming Messiah.

We too need to be very careful that there are no blinkers on our eyes, preventing us from seeing what God is saying to us. We must examine our church background and our church tradition, even where that appears good. We have to be alert to what John Stott called 'the tradition of the Evangelical elders'. We are to ensure that what we hold dear is actually biblical, and is really true and tested out.

Tradition, however noble, must not be allowed to get in the way of our obedience to God's will for us revealed in Scripture. To be truly evangelical, we need constantly to be submitting our opinions to the touchstone of God's holy Word.

The answer of Jesus to Judas' question is that *obedience to his words is the mark of a disciple who loves him*. It is only within that circle of love, composed of those who have responded to the love of God in his Son and have begun to follow him, that Jesus as king and God as Father is truly known (14:23-24). It is only as part of the community of faith that God can be experienced (14:21).

Here again is the exclusive challenge of the gospel which is folly to ignore. It is the loving Saviour who warns us that this is the case.

Then Judas (not Judas Iscariot) said, 'But, Lord, why do you intend to show yourself to us and not to the world?' [23]Jesus replied, 'If anyone loves me, he will obey my teaching. My Father will love him, and we will come to him and make our home with him. [24]He who does not love me will not obey my teaching. These words you hear are not my own; they belong to the Father who sent me...' (John 14:22-24).

There is a wonderful Trinitarian expression in these verses. Jesus says clearly that where the Son is, the Father and the Spirit are also (14:17, 23). Those who welcome Jesus find themselves related to the whole Trinity!

But Jesus delights to show more of himself to his disciples (verse 21). The work of the Spirit will constantly seek to make Jesus more real to his disciples (more about this in chapters 9 and 10). There is great joy in deepening knowledge and experience of the Lord Jesus, and our Saviour is committed to our growth. I like the comment of J. C. Ryle on verse 21: 'There is more of heaven on earth to be obtained than most Christians are aware of.'[2]

Conclusion

We have sympathised with the troubled hearts that asked the four questions and have been both encouraged and challenged by the answers Jesus gave. I believe they are so important, that I would like to summarise what we discovered.

The four questions came from confused and bewildered disciples: firstly from Peter, the loving disciple, with more spiritual ambition than strength; secondly, from Thomas, the sceptical disciple with a pessimistic bent but fiercely loyal; thirdly, the question from Philip, with a deep hunger and thirst for God, but slow on the uptake; fourthly, a question from Judas, a captive to his own upbringing. Each one loving and loyal, but confused, slow and somewhat blinkered.

My reader, is that a description of you? It certainly is of me. Yes, I love the Lord; yes, I want to be loyal to him, but sometimes I am slow on the uptake, sometimes I am

---

2. J. C. Ryle, *Expository Thoughts on the Gospel of John*.

so blinkered. As Jesus met the needs and questions of the disciples of old, he can meet ours too. He is the answer to our deepest needs.

It is interesting the way in which John has strung the four questions together as he accurately recounts what happened in the Upper Room. Four questions that run on from one another.

The first question is: *Where are you going, Jesus?* In other words: 'What is your destiny, and what is ours?' Jesus answered: 'Heaven is where I am going. I am the only way to heaven. I have come to open the door to heaven for you, so that you can enjoy my Father's house with me. Trust me with your future.'

The second question is: *How do we get there?* What's the way to heaven? Jesus answered: 'Have a relationship of trust with me and walk with me, for I am the Way.'

The third question is: *How can we experience God?* Or to express it differently: 'What shall we see and when shall we encounter God?' Jesus answered: 'I am the only one who reveals God. If you know me, you know God.'

The fourth question is: *Why reveal yourself only to your disciples?* The question means, Please help us to understand what you are up to. Jesus answered: 'Only believers in me can really know God and get to his home one day. God is redeeming a people for his own possession.'

In short, the answer to all the questions of these four troubled hearts is one word: *Jesus*. He is the answer. Jesus came to provide himself as the way to heaven. Through Jesus we experience God. It is only through Jesus that the Holy Trinity, the one true God, will make himself known to believers.

Here then is a sure hope for our lives with our troubled hearts, yes, a foundation for eternity.

SECTION 3

The Last Gift

Chapter 9

The Holy Spirit (1)
(John 14:15-31)

It is of great importance that we understand the work of the Holy Spirit from these chapters. It has been said that 25-30 years ago the Holy Spirit was the forgotten member of the Trinity. With regard to the Christian circles in which I grew up, I gladly acknowledge that there was a biblical understanding of the person and work of the Holy Spirit. But I am aware of some circles where that was not the case. However, the Charismatic renewal of the last three decades has resulted in a marked focusing on the work of the Holy Spirit, illustrating that as the theological pendulum has swung, it has swung in the opposite direction from the previous situation. Even charismatic leaders have been concerned that, in some places, all the concentration seems to be on the work of the Holy Spirit. Tom Smail wrote a book called *The Forgotten Father*[1] because he was concerned that the other two members of the Trinity, particularly the Father, were being neglected.

Therefore, it is absolutely vital that we understand Jesus' teaching in John 13-17. For it is not only precious, it is foundational. Remember, the apostles and the early disciples had this information from the lips of Jesus. What Jesus says here about the Spirit is the foundation for

---

1. Tom Smail, *The Forgotten Father*, Hodder & Stoughton.

'If you love me, you will obey what I command. [16]And I will ask the Father, and he will give you another Counsellor to be with you for ever – [17]the Spirit of truth. The world cannot accept him, because it neither sees him nor knows him. But you know him, for he lives with you and will be in you. [18]I will not leave you as orphans; I will come to you. [19]Before long, the world will not see me any more, but you will see me. Because I live, you also will live. [20]On that day you will realise that I am in my Father, and you are in me, and I am in you. [21]Whoever has my commands and obeys them, he is the one who loves me. He who loves me will be loved by my Father, and I too will love him and show myself to him.'

[22]Then Judas (not Judas Iscariot) said, 'But, Lord, why do you intend to show yourself to us and not to the world?'

[23]Jesus replied, 'If anyone loves me, he will obey my teaching. My Father will love him, and we will come to him and make our home with him. [24]He who does not love me will not obey my teaching. These words you hear are not my own; they belong to the Father who sent me.

[25]'All this I have spoken while still with you. [26]But the Counsellor, the Holy Spirit, whom the Father will send in my name, will teach you all things and will remind you of everything I have said to you. [27]Peace I leave with you; my peace I give you. I do not give to you as the world gives. Do not let your hearts be troubled and do not be afraid.

[28]'You heard me say, "I am going away and I am coming back to you." If you loved me, you would be glad that I am going to the Father, for the Father is greater than I. [29]I have told you now before it happens, so that when it does happen you will believe. [30]I will not speak with you much longer, for the prince of this world is coming. He has no hold on me, [31]but the world must learn that I love the Father and that I do exactly what my Father has commanded me. Come now; let us leave' (John 14:15-31).

rightly understanding the rest of the New Testament teaching on the third person of the Godhead. But some Christians, instead of laying an adequate foundation from these chapters, rush to other sections of the New Testament where there is teaching on the gifts of the Spirit or 'graces of the Spirit' (the 'fruit of the Spirit' in Galatians 5). But if we lay the foundation well, it will save us from making a lot of mistakes in interpreting other parts of the New Testament.

Some time ago, at a major Christian event, I shared the leadership of a late-night seminar on the work of the Spirit. It was one of the most extraordinary experiences of my Christian ministry: 1,200 people came to a 10.30 p.m. seminar that was followed by a lengthy question time. The other leaders were a brother and sister in Christ. We agreed on a lot of things; but at some points we had slight differences, and at other points we had substantial differences. Most of the substantial differences actually came back to what I would see as a lack of understanding of the teaching of Jesus in these chapters.

How important it is then that we lay the foundation that Jesus laid for the apostles.

We have seen that Jesus spoke about his relationship to the Father (John 14:8-10). So it is not surprising that he also speaks about the Holy Spirit: 'I will ask the Father and he will give you another Counsellor' (14:16); 'But the Counsellor, the Holy Spirit, whom the Father will send, in my name' (14:26). In 15:26 Jesus says he will send the Holy Spirit from the Father. The intimacy and the closeness of relationship in the Trinity between the Father, the Son and the Holy Spirit is breathtaking.

So what does Jesus teach about the Holy Spirit in this

section of the Upper Room ministry? He says that the Spirit is the ever-present Counsellor, he is the Spirit of truth, he is concerned with holiness, he is the heavenly Teacher and he is the bringer of peace. I will briefly explain the significance of each of these aspects of his work.

1. The ever-present Counsellor

'And I will ask the Father and he will give you another Counsellor, to be with you forever' (14:16).

Because these words are so familiar to us, we can very easily miss the significance of what Jesus was saying. The disciples were heartbroken that Jesus was going to leave them. So Jesus said to them, 'I am going to send you *another* Counsellor.' How does that help us to understand the Holy Spirit?

When I was first ordained, the Authorised Version of the Bible and the Prayer Book services were still widely used in the Church of England. Christians referred frequently to the Holy Spirit as the 'Holy Ghost'. In some people's minds 'the Holy Ghost' was a slightly frightening term for understanding the third person of the Trinity, because he was connected with the common use of the word 'ghost'. In other words, someone who is really frightening!

It is interesting that this is the first thing that Jesus says to troubled disciples who are beginning to anticipate his leaving them and are very upset about the prospect. When Jesus says 'I am going to send you *another* Counsellor', he is indicating that the Spirit is just like him. Just as they had appreciated the ministry of Jesus, so they would appreciate the ministry of the Spirit. The Spirit would be like the invisible presence of Jesus. Paul actually uses the title 'Spirit of Christ' to describe the Spirit (Romans 8:9).

Secondly, Jesus tells these troubled disciples that the Spirit is the *Counsellor*. 'Counsellor' is a difficult word to translate; the Greek word *parakletos* literally is 'a person called alongside'. Other translations have 'advocate' instead of the New International Version's choice of 'counsellor'. The word means somebody who is called alongside as the *counsel for the defence*. In these chapters Jesus uses several legal pictures to describe the Holy Spirit and his work. The Spirit, of course, is not somebody I am only employing in a court; he actually takes a real interest in my whole case because he is my friend and defender.

The Bible tells us that Satan is the accuser of the brethren, that he still continues to accuse us after we become Christians (Revelation 12:10). He whispers in our ears that we are worthless. He will suggest it is embarrassing for us to have to go to God repeatedly and ask forgiveness for the same sins. He will infer that because we have sinned, the Lord will stop loving us. He will attempt to make us think we have failed as Christians. His aim is to make us feel discouraged and despondent. But the Spirit of God is our Advocate who comes alongside and says to us: 'You are not worthless. You have been loved with an everlasting love. How can you believe that God, who made you in his image and sent his Son to die on the Cross (the worst kind of death) for you, would suddenly decide you are of no value? If God in eternity could plan your redemption, then he is going to bring you to the Father's house in heaven.'

The Holy Spirit is the Counsel for the Defence of the Christian. He encourages us to trust God's Word, to hold firm to his promises, to lift up our hearts and see the love of God expressed in the death of his Son.

There is a story told of a Christian who, on meeting a sad-looking friend, said to him, 'Why are you despondent? God isn't dead! Why are you cast down?' Christians should not be troubled unduly. Jesus went to the Cross to open the way to heaven for them. The Holy Spirit is the gift of the Lord Jesus to be the Counsel for their Defence.

But there is more to the Spirit's role as a counsellor. The presence of Jesus had brought the presence of the Holy Spirit and he had been present 'with' the disciples. The disciples, as Jews, would have known Old Testament passages where the Holy Spirit came upon people to enable them to fulfil God's purpose. But here is a distinctive privilege of the New Covenant, a privilege that is superior to what was experienced by believers under the Old Covenant. Jesus says of the Spirit: 'for he lives with you and will be *in* you' (14:17).

Jesus is stressing that God is going to be even closer to the disciples than he was when the Lord Jesus was present with them. Sometimes we think: 'I would have loved to have been a disciple when Jesus was here.' But in John 16:7 Jesus says to his disciples, 'It is for your good that I am going away.' There are a number of reasons why he says that and we will look at these later. But one of the reasons is that God was going to come closer to them than he had actually been during the previous three years of Jesus' presence. Can I put it like this? God could not come any closer! What an amazing, precious privilege that is.

'I will ask the Father and he will give you another Counsellor to be with you *for ever*' (14:16).

I am an incurable romantic at heart; therefore I always notice romantic adverts. I was particularly taken by the advert that had the catch phrase, 'a diamond is for ever'. A diamond is the most precious gift we can give in a matrimonial sense. But the Holy Spirit is a far more precious gift from the Lord Jesus to the disciples. He is a *for ever* gift from Jesus. The Holy Spirit was not to be given to the disciples and then withdrawn. Our relationship with him is not broken the way some engagements or marriages are.

Christian, how can you be troubled? How can you be fearful or afraid? Of course, from time to time as we face the challenges of life, we will be troubled. But we have good reason to lift up our hearts. God has come as near as he could possibly come, he has taken up residence inside us. The powerful Spirit of God, the *Ruach Adonai* who breathed over the waters and created the world (Genesis 1:2), who is the invisible presence of Jesus, has taken up residence in our hearts.

We have the resources to face anything in life because we have the presence of Jesus with us. I remember the time, when as a university student, the truth of this really came home to me. I was worried about a final exam paper. As I went up the steps to the exam hall on a hot day (like today as I write!), I thought, 'Even if I don't pass this exam I am one of the few people who is going into this hall with the living God with me.' (There were about 2,000 students.)

We have seen then that Jesus has two answers for troubled hearts. First, his disciples are to focus their attention on heaven (14:1-4). Second, before they arrive in heaven they will have the permanent presence of the Holy Spirit as the Counsellor. Jesus would not abandon them, he would not leave them as orphans (14:18). He would stand by them in all the troubles of life. A friend of mine likes to put it this way: 'Being a Christian is not just pie in the sky when you die, it's steak on the plate while you wait!'

2. The Spirit of truth

Jesus describes the Holy Spirit as 'the Spirit of truth' (14:17). Obviously, then, the Holy Spirit is concerned about truth and truthfulness. Truth is a great theme of John's Gospel.

Remember the story of the woman at the well (John 4). When the discussion with Jesus was getting too hot for her, she asked him a theological question to take the spotlight off the potency of his line of discussion with her about her husbands. Jesus replied by saying:

'Yet a time is coming and has now come when the true worshippers will worship the Father in spirit and in *truth*, for they are the kind of worshippers the Father seeks. God is spirit, and his worshippers must worship in spirit and in *truth*' (4:23, 24).

You will recall too that John records this statement that Jesus said in the Upper Room:

'I am the way and *the truth* and the life. No-one comes to the Father except through me' (John 14:6).

I don't know if you have thought about those three statements in John 14:6. Because they are so familiar it is very easy not to think about them. If any of the statements is to the fore in comparison with the other two, it is 'I am the truth'. John 1:1-18 lays out in embryo everything that John will say in his Gospel. In verse 18, he says: 'No-one has ever seen God, but God the only Son, who is at the Father's side, has made him known.' Why is Jesus the only way to the Father? Because he is the only one who reveals the truth about God. He actually *is* the truth. He is the one who was at the Father's side and is therefore capable of revealing the truth about God. And because he is the truth, he is the only way.

Does Jesus mean that all philosophical truth is wrapped up in him? No! What he means is that all the truth about God, about human nature, about our need, about the possibility of a relationship with God, about how we can be saved and forgiven and get to heaven and share the Father's house, is in Jesus. All the truth that is important and fundamental is wrapped up in Jesus. We can never know the truth about how and why the world happened, apart from Christ. We can never know the truth about our own human nature and deeper needs, apart from Jesus. We can never know the truth about God and have life in him, apart from Christ. Because he is the truth, a relationship with him will bring us to see the truth about ourselves and about our world, and about God.

So if the Father wishes to be worshipped in truth, the Son is the One who must reveal the Father. It is not surprising then that the Holy Spirit is the 'Spirit of truth'. There is right through John's Gospel *a Trinitarian concern for truth*. The Spirit of truth is given to lead people to the One who is the truth.

Jesus says in verse 17 that 'the world cannot accept

him because it neither sees him nor knows him'. The 'world' in John's Gospel is the whole of human society in rebellion against their Maker. The world cannot see God because it will not face the truth about itself, it will not face the truth about the Lord Jesus. In a very real sense, a person who has not been found by Christ and discovered the truth in him is living a lie! That is very different from what the average person thinks, if they ever think about what Christianity is. At best, Christianity is seen by some as a means of making life more interesting or tolerable. But becoming a Christian is not escapism, it is facing the truth about ourselves and our world and God for the first time.

I said earlier that the Spirit of truth is concerned about truth and truthfulness. The Spirit will not propagate lies. His ministry will help us to face the truth, however uncomfortable that may be for ourselves. His ministry will also encourage Christians to tell the truth and to be truthful people.

I say this with a sense of sadness because I have observed among Christians a deterioration in the standard of telling the truth. It is amazing how many white lies are told. But there is no such thing as a 'white' lie. Lack of truth among Christians can take different forms. Sometimes it can be used to get out of an awkward situation. At times it can be used to flatter someone (flattery is sometimes a middle class and respectable way of being untruthful). There are many ways in which we can be economical with the truth. The Spirit of Truth wants believers to practise the truth as they follow the One who is the truth.

3. The *Holy* Spirit

In verse 25, the Spirit of truth is called the *Holy* Spirit. In other words he is concerned about holiness. It is certainly true of much modern Christianity that there is not the same concern for holiness as there once was.[2]

Why is it that holiness has become an unpopular word among Christians? Is it because holiness has become associated with being 'so heavenly minded that we are no earthly good'? Some imagine holiness as being similar to a stained glass window where the saint hovers a few feet above the ground and looks beautiful and saintly but does not have any contact with reality! Could it be that holiness is associated, even subconsciously in some evangelical minds who think they have long since abandoned that type of thinking, with that kind of removal from the world? But the requirement of the Lord for his people to be holy as he is holy has not changed. This major concern of the Lord for his own people ought to be our concern.

We have all known people who have confused 'uprightness' with 'uptightness', the kind of behaviour that can give holiness a bad name. But holiness, in its biblical sense, means being 'set apart' for the Lord to belong to him. It includes serving and worshipping him out of thankfulness for all that he has given us in the Lord Jesus Christ. Redeemed by his love, we, his children, are set apart to be distinct and different in his world. But we are not to be awkward and angular. We are not to be 'weird' different, but to be 'special' different from a world in rebellion against its Maker.

---

2. In the early 1990s there has been a resurgence of books about holiness. In my opinion, the most outstanding is *A Passion for Holiness* by J. I. Packer, published by Crossway.

The Holy Spirit's concern, in producing holiness in us, is to encourage us to be real in the service of our Lord, even if it results in us being members of an unpopular minority. What does that mean in practice? It means that the Holy Spirit will put his finger on every area of our lives that needs dealing with.

When I was an unmarried Curate in Cheadle, I first lived in a very cold house that was much too big for my needs. It was a lovely house and when it was finally renovated and had central heating and double glazing installed it was super. But initially it was freezing and I used to go to bed at night with eight blankets just to keep warm, and I would get up in the morning totally exhausted by the weight of them! I never even opened certain parts of the house. One Spring, my Mum was coming on a visit. My Mum was the kind of lady who (so went the family joke) would go round with a duster in her hand waiting for the dust to fall! I knew I was going to be in big trouble if the house wasn't up to scratch. I ventured into the spare bedroom which I had left for the winter with the curtains closed. When I pulled back the curtains, to my horror I saw just how bad the room had become! There were cobwebs, there was dust, it needed a thorough spring-clean.

Sometimes new Christians say to me: 'Do you know, I feel worse than before I became a Christian! Why is it, Wallace, that I feel worse?' My response always is, 'You feel worse because God has pulled back the curtains of your dirty room, and he has let the light of his presence shine into it. When you begin to see some of the things that you never noticed before about yourself, thank God that he has pulled back the curtains. Thank him that he is beginning to do a spring-cleaning work in your life which will one day be completed when he brings you to glory. Praise him! It is for your good he has pulled back the curtains.'

There is always at least one area of our lives in which each of us is not keen to let the Lord have his way. Maybe it is our finance, maybe how we are as a parent or a partner, maybe it is our business interests or leisure activities. The Holy Spirit, in one way or another, will constantly be showing us areas of our lives that we need to put right – even when we don't want him to. For the *Holy* Spirit is concerned about our holiness.

Once I lived in temporary accommodation for about three months. A kind couple gave me accommodation on the top floor of a four-storey house. My landlord told me on the day I arrived: 'Look, we do want you to understand that you live on the top floor. You can come down and use the lounge when we are out, if you ask permission beforehand. And you must never use the bathroom on the second floor. It is out of limits ...' At the end of three months I didn't feel very much at home! The terms of my landlord illustrate how there can be areas of our lives that we try and keep the Lord out of. But the Holy Spirit is not a temporary tenant. He will constantly knock on the door of that room until we let him have access.

4. The heavenly Teacher
In 14:26 Jesus said that 'the Counsellor, the Holy Spirit, whom the Father will send in my name, will teach you all things and will remind you of everything I have said to you'. I don't know how many teachers will read this book! What is clear is that there is no Christian learning

apart from the work of the Holy Spirit. The Holy Spirit wants us to learn and his aim is to teach.

We don't often hear the Holy Spirit described as the Teacher, and yet that is the fourth of the great descriptions of the Holy Spirit on the lips of the Lord Jesus here as he is teaching the disciples about the work of the Spirit. A friend said to me on one occasion, 'There are no graduates in the school of Christ! We don't graduate until we get to glory.' On this side of glory the Holy Spirit as our teacher will encourage us as God's children to become mature. All our lives we will remain disciples in the school of Christ, and disciples are meant to be good learners.

Primarily, verse 26 is a promise made to the apostles. As we go through John 14-17, we need to recognise that there are some promises made to every Christian, but there are other promises made specifically to the apostles. For example, verse 12 is a promise to all believers: 'I tell you the truth, *anyone* who has faith in me will do what I have been doing.' Admittedly, the verse has been greatly misused and misunderstood. But it is a general promise to anyone who has faith. But verse 26 is a *particular* promise to those in the Upper Room.

However, the statement of verse 26 does raise some very important questions. How did the apostles record reliably all that Jesus said throughout those three years? Can we trust the New Testament as reliable? Can we believe it is the Word of Truth and the Word of God, a total and completely reliable witness to the revelation of God in Christ? The answer to such questions is that the Holy Spirit would be given to the apostles, to remind them what to write down for our learning.

Jesus was sometimes called 'Rabbi'. His disciples

learned by the rabbinic method of instruction: hearing repeatedly the same things, although sometimes in different circumstances and with different illustrations. They would have been expected to remember and repeat what they had learned. So in a human sense the circumstances were the right setting to remember and write down accurately what Jesus had said to them.

But it was not just a human situation. The Holy Spirit would be given to them to enable them to remember what Jesus had said to them. So verse 26 is a particular promise to the apostles in the Upper Room, for which you and I ought to be amazingly grateful.

Please notice two very important guidelines that Jesus gave concerning the teaching ministry of the Spirit.

First, Jesus clearly said that the teaching ministry of the Holy Spirit would be a reminding one. There is a lot of emphasis today on 'new' things that the Spirit is saying. Indeed, the claim is often made that the Holy Spirit puts new thoughts directly into people's minds. But the teaching ministry of the Holy Spirit is a reminding one. In other words, the Holy Spirit, who loves to magnify Jesus, would bring the apostles, and indeed all his disciples, back to the teaching of Jesus, back to what Jesus said and did.

Secondly, the Holy Spirit teaches by drawing out the significance of what Jesus said and did. Look at John 16:14: 'He will bring glory to me by taking from what is mine and making it known to you.' After the cross, resurrection and ascension of Jesus and following his own coming at Pentecost, the Holy Spirit would remind the apostles of what Jesus had taught them, and help them to see the significance of what Jesus had said and done.

Judas asked a very interesting question in verse 22 – a question whose significance is often missed. He saw the point of what Jesus was saying. He realised that the coming of the Messiah would result in a new world order. Therefore, he was stunned by the exclusiveness of what Jesus was teaching. Jesus had been explaining how he is the only way for believers to know the Father. The point was not lost on Judas who asked, 'Lord, why do you intend to show yourself to us and not to the world?' (verse 22). Jesus answered, 'If anyone loves me he will obey my teaching. My Father will love him and we will come to him and make our home with him' (verse 23). Isn't that terrific? Not only is there the Father's house in heaven for those who open themselves to the Lord Jesus Christ as Saviour, but the Father and the Son, by the presence of the Spirit, are making their home now in the lives of obedient believers. That's the bottom line. It is only to those who obey Jesus' teaching that the persons of the Trinity make themselves known.

This interesting but essential aspect of Christ's teaching is highlighted in verses 22 and 23. In verse 23 Jesus says that 'If anyone loves me, he will *obey* my teaching'. In verse 24, Jesus teaches that any 'who does not love me will *not obey* my teaching'. We can safely conclude that the aim of the Holy Spirit is to instruct disciples how to obey the teaching of Jesus (verse 26).

It is important to stress that the Holy Spirit teaches by reminding of what has been revealed. My wife and I were at a conference recently. One morning we listened to a superb exposition of Isaiah 53 that moved us to tears as we thought of the wonder of the love of Christ for us. Yet afterwards someone got up and said, 'I wonder what the *now* word from the Lord is for us today.' We had just had the *now* word of the Lord for the previous 45 minutes!

It is the constant delight of the Holy Spirit, who loves to magnify Jesus, to bring all believers back to the apostolic testimony to the Lord Jesus, and then to draw out *the significance* of what Jesus said and did, so that he might apply it to their hearts. The Holy Spirit *speaks* by taking us back to what *has* being spoken.

I wonder how seriously we are taking the Holy Spirit's work as the heavenly Teacher. We need to be reminded continually of biblical truths. How do we hear God speak infallibly today? By the Spirit bringing us back to Scripture. This will involve listening to sermons, going to Bible studies with other believers, and applying personally what we read in the Scriptures.

But those who are called to teach the Word of God also need to be dependent, as they teach the Word of God, on the one who is the Teacher. Amongst such, there needs to be a radical daily dependence on the Holy Spirit to enable them to teach the Word of God truthfully and with proper application. Believers should pray that those who teach the Scriptures will depend on the Holy Spirit to enable them to teach afresh the living Word of God – for that is what it is.

5. The bringer of peace

The Holy Spirit is not mentioned specifically in 14:27, but in context is clearly linked with the gift of peace. He is the bringer of peace. The peace of God is inevitably associated with the gift of the Spirit, as can be seen from John 20:19-22:

> On the evening of that first day of the week, when the disciples were together, with the doors locked for fear of the Jews, Jesus came and stood among them and said, 'Peace be with you!' After he said this, he showed them his hands and side. The disciples were overjoyed when they saw the Lord.
>
> Again Jesus said, 'Peace be with you! As the Father has sent me, I am sending you.' And with that he breathed on them and said, 'Receive the Holy Spirit.'

On that occasion on the Resurrection day, the first thing that Jesus gave the disciples was peace. But the gift of peace was associated there with the gift of the Spirit.

And in John 14:27 it is in the context of describing the work of the Spirit that Jesus talks about his peace. Jesus is certainly referring to peace with God which is made possible by his death on our behalf. It was after his death and resurrection that Jesus said to his disciples, 'Peace be with you.' He had won for them peace with God. So peace with God is a gift to every child of God.

But in verse 27 Jesus specifically says 'my peace'. It is not just peace with God that is meant, it is also the peace *of* Christ. I think that the peace of Christ is the joyful certainty that we are God's children and are safe in his hands. It is knowing we are justified and adopted into his family on the basis of what Jesus did for us. We now belong to him and are loved by him. He is in control of everything, therefore we need not be anxious.

That peacefulness of relationship between Jesus and his Father which was so manifest in his life, he has won for us and will give to us as his disciples. Let me explain what this means.

Look back to John 13:3: 'Jesus knew that the Father

had put all things under his power and that he had come
from God and was returning to God.' In the confidence of
his own relationship to God and who he was and what
God had sent him to do, he then ministers to his disciples
and shows them his love. That relationship of peace
between the Father and the Son, which had been so
obvious to the disciples during the three years of his
public ministry, would be won for them by Jesus through
his death. Just as Jesus was secure in his Father's love and
care for him, so they, in a sense, could be secure in the
knowledge of his love for them.

What I am describing is the daily application of the
peace of God, that has been won for us on the Cross. We
are God's children; we are loved by him; we belong to
him; we are on the way to glory under his care; he will
never leave us or forsake us. That joyful, delightful
certainty, that peace of Christ, is the day-by-day birth-
right of every Christian. It is the Holy Spirit's delight, as
well as his work, to lead his people to rejoice in Jesus and
to know the peace and security and delight of the fact that
they are in their Father's hands, under his control and on
the way to heaven! The ministry of the Holy Spirit is to
bring to us the benefits of the death of Christ. J. I. Packer,
in his excellent book *Keep in Step with the Spirit*, says that
'essentially the work of the Spirit is not about power or
performance or purity but about mediating to us the
presence of Jesus'.[3]

---

3. J. I. Packer, *Keep in Step with the Spirit*, IVP, 1984.

Heaven on earth

In verse 18, Jesus reminded his disciples that he would not leave them as orphans, but that he would come to them. I think that Jesus was there referring to two distinct comings. The first is described in verse 19: 'before long, the world will not see me any more', by which he meant his death. 'But you will see me' describes his appearances to his disciples after his resurrection. 'Because I live you also will live' means that his resurrection is the vindication of what he did for them. On the day of his resurrection the disciples would know that they are loved by him. Jesus was not going to leave them as orphans. The resurrection would convince them of that!

In verse 21, Jesus described a second kind of coming: 'Whoever has my commands and obeys them, he is the one who loves me. He who loves me will be loved by my Father, and I too will love him and show myself to him.' Here is an open statement that can apply to any believer, whether they were a witness of the resurrection or not.

Verse 21 details Jesus' coming to disciples who are loving him and obeying him, and so deepening their knowledge of him and their delight in him. Although some Christians grossly exaggerate what we can have this side of heaven – full health and full wealth – we must not overreact and miss what Jesus promises. This is a promise of getting to know him better – of knowing him in a deeper and a richer way.

How does that come about? It comes about through the Holy Spirit deepening our love for Jesus and our knowledge of him. This is how J. C. Ryle put it: 'There is more of heaven on earth to be obtained than most Christians are aware of.' We need to rejoice in and experience this aspect of the promise of Jesus to us.

The disciples who were fearful of being left as orphans would still know the presence of Jesus with them; the Holy Spirit, the Counsellor, would be with them and in them for ever. The disciples of Jesus do not belong to an orphanage; they are the King's sons who are the beneficiaries of all that the Son of God has won for them!

Chapter 10

The Holy Spirit (2)
(John 15:26-27; 16:5-16)

We have seen already that the Holy Spirit is the Counsel for the Defence of Christians, who is called alongside believers to defend them against the accusations of the evil one. The Counsellor is 'another one like Jesus' who would carry on the ministry of Jesus to the disciples. God would come nearer because the Spirit, the distinctive mark of the New Covenant, would be in them.

Every time that Jesus introduces material about the Holy Spirit he repeats the word 'Counsellor' first of all (14:15; 14:26; 15:26; 16:7). As Christians we are accustomed to refer to the Spirit as the Holy Spirit which, of course, is biblical and right. But Jesus spoke about the Spirit as the Advocate, as the Counsellor, as the one who is in place of him and who is just like him. Perhaps more Christians would have less worries and uncertainties and vaguenesses about the Holy Spirit if they followed the example of Jesus and got it clearly in their minds that he is like Jesus. He is there to be with his people, to be their defence, to be the presence of Jesus with them as they follow Christ.

The Character Witness for Jesus
In a courtroom it is very important for someone on trial to produce character witnesses who know them well and can

'When the Counsellor comes, whom I will send to you from the Father, the Spirit of truth who goes out from the Father, he will testify about me; [27]but you also must testify, for you have been with me from the beginning.'

[5]'Now I am going to him who sent me, yet none of you asks me, "Where are you going?" [6]Because I have said these things, you are filled with grief. [7]But I tell you the truth: It is for your good that I am going away. Unless I go away, the Counsellor will not come to you; but if I go, I will send him to you. [8]When he comes, he will convict the world of guilt in regard to sin and righteousness and judgment: [9]in regard to sin, because men do not believe in me; [10]in regard to righteousness, because I am going to the Father, where you can see me no longer; [11]and in regard to judgment, because the prince of this world now stands condemned.

[12]'I have much more to say to you, more than you can now bear. [13]But when he, the Spirit of truth, comes, he will guide you into all truth. He will not speak on his own; he will speak only what he hears, and he will tell you what is yet to come. [14]He will bring glory to me by taking from what is mine and making it known to you. [15]All that belongs to the Father is mine. That is why I said the Spirit will take from what is mine and make it known to you.

[16]'In a little while you will see me no more, and then after a little while you will see me' (John 15:26-27; 16:5-16).

speak up for them. Notice what Jesus says here about the Holy Spirit: 'When the Counsellor comes, whom I will send to you from the Father, he will testify about me' (15:26). Back in 14:15, he had said: 'I will ask the Father and he will give you another Counsellor'; the Spirit comes from the Father. Here in 15:26 the Spirit comes from the Father but is sent by the Son. It is interesting how the persons of the Trinity co-operate and their roles overlap!

The 'He' in 'He will testify about me' is literally 'that one'; in Greek the word is not neuter but masculine. The Spirit of God is a 'he' not an 'it'. The Bible reveals the Holy Spirit is a *person*. Yet even in evangelical circles, I have heard the Holy Spirit referred to as 'it'. Some illustrate the filling of the Holy Spirit as being similar to a tumbler filling up with water. But the Holy Spirit is not a commodity within us that needs to be topped up. One cannot get a bit of a person, then a bit more some time later. If we want to be filled with the Holy Spirit, then it is not realised by us having more of him, but by him having more of us – by his influence being more real in us.

The Holy Spirit's delight is ever to be pointing people to Jesus and leading people to praise him. It is as if he stands up in a courtroom and says, 'I want to tell you about Jesus. He is wonderful! He is who he claims to be. He did what God sent him to do. He died that you might be forgiven.' The Spirit will testify to Jesus.

One of the most helpful comments I have ever read on the work of the Holy Spirit is by J. I. Packer. He writes about the 'floodlight' or the 'spotlight' ministry of the Holy Spirit.[1] It is an analogy that means a lot to me. In the

1. J. I. Packer, *Keep in Step with the Spirit*, IVP, 1984.

previous church in which I worked, the building was very old and beautiful, dating from 1325. I can remember coming from a Christmas service, and it was a real Christmas card scene. The church and the ground all around were covered in snow. The floodlights were on and it looked absolutely magnificent. Being romantic I like things like that! In fact, I went home and said to my wife, 'Come and have a look at the church.' I thought it looked so beautiful, I actually put my boots on and went back out to have another look!

What does a floodlight do? It doesn't say 'Look at me', does it? The purpose of a floodlight or a spotlight is to point away from itself to the object that it is highlighting and magnifying. The Holy Spirit's desire is to magnify Jesus, to point away from himself and to say 'look at Jesus'.

If we are to get our basic thinking straight about the work of the Spirit, then any claimed work of the Spirit that constantly points, as it were, to the Spirit magnifying himself and saying, 'The Spirit, the Spirit' to the neglect of Jesus, is unlikely to be the genuine work of the Spirit. For the genuine work of the Holy Spirit wants to flood-light Jesus. Do you see the point? The Holy Spirit, if I may put it like this, is self-effacing and Jesus-glorifying.

The author and help of all testimony about Jesus
The Holy Spirit wants *us* to magnify Jesus. Look what Jesus says: 'he will testify about me; but you also must testify for you have been with me from the beginning' (15:26, 27). It is a particular command to the apostles for they were eyewitnesses of Jesus' life, death and resurrec-tion. When they later replaced Judas Iscariot with Mat-

thias, one of the qualifications for apostleship was someone who had been with them from the beginning and who
also was an eyewitness of the life, death and resurrection
of the Lord Jesus (Acts 1:21-22). So by very definition,
there cannot be that type of apostle today. There may be
apostles in a secondary sense, in the etymological sense
of 'a sent one from God', or someone gifted as a church
planter. But in the sense of the Twelve, in the sense of the
foundation of the church (Ephesians 2:20), there cannot
be apostles today. They were called to be a particular
foundation witness which would remain the foundation
of the church in every generation. They were called to
testify to Christ.

But the whole church too has been commissioned to
testify to the risen Christ. And in verse 27 we see the
promise of the Holy Spirit as the source and the help of all
testimony about Jesus. Here is a call for the church to bear
witness, but also a promise from the lips of Jesus of the
help to carry out that witness. There is a lovely balance
between obedience and dependence. Jesus knew it
wouldn't always be easy to witness to him; words would
be hard, sometimes situations would be difficult, relationships might be strained, embarrassment could be
caused. When believers realise their inadequacy and
inability to witness in their own strength, the Holy Spirit
helps them to testify. But Jesus, as he calls them to face
what it means to live in the real world and to follow him
obediently, gives all that they need in order to carry out
their witness for him. The Holy Spirit is both the character
witness for Jesus and the encourager of all who want to
praise Jesus. The Spirit is our resource and he is our
enabler.

Some people want to experience the Holy Spirit and to know his power. But the Holy Spirit comes to enable Christians to testify to their Saviour, and to live for him. Therefore, unless we have a heart to testify to him we will not know the Holy Spirit's enabling power.

Let me illustrate this from Acts 4:23-31. Peter and John were told that they would be in great danger from the civil authorities if they went on testifying about Jesus. Remember their Master had been crucified by the joint co-operation of the religious and civil rulers. On their release (verse 23) Peter and John went back to their own people and reported all that the chief priests and elders had said to them. 'When they heard this, they raised their voices together in prayer' (verse 24). They are under threat, so *their first reaction is to pray*. What a perspective they had on the situation! Would that the church today, when up against it and in danger, would always have the same reaction.

But look at their grip on who God is and their estimation of his Word: 'Sovereign Lord ... you made the heaven and the earth ... you spoke by the Holy Spirit through the mouth of your servant, our father David ...' (verses 24-25). They knew God was in control of all events: 'Indeed Herod and Pontius Pilate met together with the Gentiles and the people of Israel in this city to conspire against your holy servant Jesus, whom you anointed. They did what your power and will decided beforehand should happen' (verses 27-28).

Do you know how the message of victory at Waterloo came across the English Channel? All of Britain waited to see what the outcome of the battle was, because if Wellington had lost the battle, Europe would have been overrun by Napoleon. Slowly the message came through by semaphore and it began 'Wellington defeated'. The hearts sank of those who saw it. But then the full message said 'Wellington defeated Napoleon'. On the first Good Friday, the message seemed to be 'Jesus defeated'. But the whole message of the Easter story is 'Jesus defeated Satan, and all the powers of darkness. He accomplished God's redemption for us.'

The disciples then saw that all that Jesus claimed about himself was perfectly true. The Resurrection was the vindication of all that Jesus said, and of all that he did on the Cross. He has been vindicated by his Father who raised him from the dead. He is now the living, reigning Lord and there is nothing more important in life than him! Because the early church realised this, they wanted, more than anything else, to obey his final command to go into all the world and make disciples of all nations (Matthew 28:19).

Sometimes people ask me, How can I be filled with the Holy Spirit? Acts 4 tells us the kind of people who are filled by the Holy Spirit. They are those who know Jesus is the living Lord and that nothing is more important than obedience to his commands. The Christians in Acts 4 did not pray for deliverance, but for boldness to witness for Jesus (verse 29). What would you have included in your prayer if you had been in that situation? I'll tell you what I would have included: 'Get us out of this mess!', or at the very best it would have been: 'Protect us!' The nearest these early Christians got to that type of prayer request is verse 29: 'Lord, consider their threats.' It was not their own personal peace and affluence that they were concerned about. They were concerned about what Jesus told them to do – to testify to him. So what they asked was: 'Enable your servants to speak your word with great boldness' (verse 29b). Those who realise who Jesus is, and whose heart's desire is to follow him and obey his commands, depend upon him and say to him, 'Lord, we can't do it ourselves.' And what does Jesus do? He does what he promised; he sends the Holy Spirit to help. The kind of people who are filled by the Holy Spirit are those who know who Jesus is and what he did for them, and long above everything else to obey him. When the disciples wanted help to fulfil Jesus' command to testify, they went to Jesus, expecting him to keep his promise to send his Holy Spirit. And as we seek to testify we can be dependant upon the help and the strength of the Holy Spirit. He is the author and help of all testimony about Jesus. The Holy Spirit loves to magnify Jesus.

In John 16:5, Jesus says, 'Now I am going to him who sent me, yet none of you asks me, "Where are you going?"' Jesus is picking up themes that he has already mentioned. If you look back at 14:28, you will see that he picks up from there the theme of his departure. Indeed he goes back to the question that began the whole discussion with Peter, 'Lord, where are you going?' (13:36). This time he continues, 'Because I have said these things, you are filled with grief.' The disciples thought that they would have to face the challenges of living in the real world without Jesus. Therefore they were distressed. So Jesus assures them that he has made every provision for their needs.

Verse 7 is a remarkable comment to grief-laden disciples who, because they are still distressed and troubled, are not seeing all that clearly yet. Jesus, with great care and very profound love, says to them: 'But I tell you the truth. It is for your good that I am going away.' When Jesus wanted to say something of considerable importance he would say, 'I tell you the truth.' Now there are at least three reasons why it would be good for the disciples if Jesus went away.

Firstly, his going was the means of opening the gateway to heaven for them. His going to death was the means whereby their entrance to his Father's house was accomplished.

Secondly, his going will clear the way for the Holy Spirit to come and dwell in them. He has been with them but would now be in them. As I said in the previous chapter, this is a distinctive mark of the New Covenant.

Thirdly, God would be coming as close to them as he could. The work of the Kingdom would be both deepened and broadened by the indwelling presence of the Holy Spirit. That, I take it, is what 14:12 means (a verse about which there is much discussion and I believe a great deal of misunderstanding): 'I tell you the truth, anyone who has faith in me will do what I have been doing. He will do even greater things than these, because I am going to the Father.' To help understand what Jesus means, note what he says in John 6:28: 'Then they asked him, "What must we do to do the works that God requires?" Jesus answered, "The work of God is this: to believe in the one he has sent." ' Jesus says that believing in him is the work God requires. Therefore, when Jesus speaks about doing greater works, he means that more people would come to believe in him. Jesus did not mean that the disciples would do greater miracles than he did. It is not greater things *in degree*, but it is greater things *in extent*. The

ministry of the Kingdom would go throughout the world.
The presence of Jesus would not be limited to being
physically with the disciples in one place. By the indwelling of the Holy Spirit he would be with them wherever
they went and greater things would be done in the name
of the Kingdom. More people would come to believe in
him.

For these reasons it was indeed for their good that he
was going away. And it would also be for the good of the
Lord Jesus. In a lovely, very personal comment Jesus says
in John 14:28: 'If you loved me, you would be glad that
I am going to the Father, for the Father is greater than I.'
Jesus is not implying that he is not equal with the Father.
Don Carson has an excellent and helpful comment on
this: 'Jesus is returning to the place where the Father is
undiminished in glory, unquestionably greater than the
Son in his *incarnate state* (italics mine).'[2] Jesus was
looking forward to going to the Father.

The Counsel for the Prosecution
We have seen that Jesus uses law court analogies to
describe the work of the Holy Spirit. The first and
favourite analogy of Jesus was that the Holy Spirit is the
Counsellor. He is the Counsel for the Defence of Christians, the one who is called alongside to befriend and
support and defend believers. He is 'another Counsellor'
just like Jesus. Then we saw that the Holy Spirit is the
Character Witness for Jesus. He loves to spotlight Jesus
and magnify him and lead us to praise him and testify to
him.

Next we see in verse 8 that the Holy Spirit is the

2. D. A. Carson, *The Gospel According to John*, IVP, 1991, p.508.

Counsel for the Prosecution :'When he comes, he will convict the world of guilt in regard to sin and righteousness and judgement.' No doubt the disciples, if they were thinking clearly at all, would have wondered how their testimony would carry conviction in the absence of Jesus? The answer of Jesus is that not only is the Holy Spirit the one who delights to magnify the Lord Jesus, and the author and help of all testimony about Jesus, but he is the one who carries with that testimony his convicting power. He accomplishes his work of convicting of sin, of righteousness and of judgment through the testimony of the apostles and the disciples (16:8). The Spirit will convict and convince people of three things.

First, he will convince sinners of *their guilt of personal sin*. There is no knowledge of sinfulness apart from the work of the Holy Spirit. It is the Holy Spirit working in our sinful hearts that brings us to a point of saying, 'Yes, I am guilty before a holy God'; of cutting away the pretence, the self-importance and the arrogance which is true of each sinful human heart. The Spirit works to bring sinners to see the truth about themselves, and their desperate need of a Saviour. Today, in our western society, if there is a problem it is always someone else's fault. The Holy Spirit opens us up to the uncomfortable truth that the problem is not with others, the problem is essentially with *me*.

When I was newly ordained as a curate in a church in Merseyside we had a big civic service. Two important local dignitaries attended. After the service the vicar spoke to the wife and I spoke to her husband. I said, 'It is very nice to have you and your wife here with us today.' His response was, 'I am deeply offended by the service I have just been part of.' The vicar was an excellent preacher, and as I thought there was nothing wrong with the service I felt the problem must be me! So I said to him, 'I am very sorry if I have offended you in any way.' He said, 'Oh no, it's not you in particular, although you are part of it! It's the whole thing. The opening sentence of the service said that we are all sinners. I am not a sinner. But I have been put on the same level as those in the local prison. And I am not on the same level. I don't lie or cheat or steal or murder. I am not a sinner, and I don't like being told that I am!' Boy, was he arrogant! I don't often do this, but I summoned myself up to my full 5 feet 8 inches and, tapping him on the chest, I said, 'I have news for you. You and I are both rotten sinners and in need of the mercy and grace of Christ.' It had a sobering effect on him and we had an interesting conversation afterwards!

You see, conviction of personal sin does not come by education or human wisdom, it comes from the Holy Spirit. The reason any of us sees our sinfulness before God and our need of Christ is because of the work of the Holy Spirit. The heart of sin is unbelief: 'In regard to sin because men do not believe in me' (16:9). To quote Don Carson, 'Sin is multi-faced, spiritual blindness supremely displayed in its treatment of Jesus.'[3]

Secondly, the Holy Spirit brings conviction that *righteousness cannot be earned and that it cannot be found anywhere else but in Jesus*: 'In regard to righteousness because I am going to the Father, where you can see me no longer' (16:10). This is a difficult but tremendous phrase to grasp hold of. We might have expected Jesus to say, 'In regard to righteousness because I am going to the

---

3. D. A. Carson, *The Gospel According to John*, IVP, 1991, p.538.

Cross.' But Jesus says, '... because I am going to the Father, where you can see me no longer' (16:10). There is no way for us to be right before a holy God other than through Jesus going to glory to open the way for us. The only way that he could do that for us was to go to glory via the Cross. Sometimes in John's Gospel the Cross itself is portrayed as the centre of the glory of Christ. At other times it is the whole package: the work of Christ on the Cross, the vindication of his work by his resurrection, and the welcoming back into heaven of the ascended, triumphant Lord.

Therefore, it is not surprising that Jesus phrases verse 10 the way he does. There is no way to be righteous before God and get to the Father's house except through what Jesus did on our behalf. I love the way the Puritans used to explain this point. They used to talk graphically about the 'sweet exchange'! On Jesus, the holy and righteous Son of God, was placed all our unrighteousness, and in exchange he gave us his righteousness so that as we stand before God we stand complete in that righteousness. It is the Holy Spirit who brings conviction that there is the possibility of being right before God in no other way than through the work of Christ on our behalf, and our acceptance of that by faith.

Thirdly, the Holy Spirit brings conviction about *our having to answer to God at the judgment seat*. Apart from being in Christ, we would be on the losing side on the Day of Judgment. By the Cross Jesus has defeated all the powers of darkness, all his foes: 'the prince of this world now stands condemned' (16:11).

Consider Romans 1:32: 'Although they know God's righteous decree that those who do such things deserve death ...'. That verse states clearly that the heart of man senses that he is accountable to God. The Holy Spirit magnifies that already deeply-ingrained reality in our conscience which we try to suppress, and brings to us the realisation that we must answer to God one day. When a person realises that he or she is going to have to stand before God, and face divine judgement for the things he or she has done, that conviction comes by the Holy Spirit, as the gospel is shared with them.

Indeed there is an interesting outline of the gospel proclaimed by the early disciples in these verses:

> Sin (People's need as rebels before a holy God);
> Righteousness (God's provision for our need by the death of his Son);
> Judgement (Deliverance from ruin and hell only through the mercy and love of Jesus).

The Guide

'I have much more to say to you, more than you can now bear. But when he, the Spirit of truth, comes, he will guide you into all truth. He will not speak on his own; he will speak only what he hears, and he will tell you what is yet to come' (16:12-13). What is the meaning of the phrase 'he will tell you' or literally 'he will proclaim to you what is yet to come'?

Calvin thought that Jesus meant 'the future state of his spiritual Kingdom'.[4] In other words, what would happen between the first coming of the Lord Jesus (and his return to heaven and to glory) and his second coming. John Stott offers a helpful comment on this: 'Maybe it refers to

---

4. John Calvin, *Commentary on John*, Vol. 2, p.120.

Christ's coming death, resurrection, ascension and gift of the Holy Spirit as well as to his return at the end of time.'[5]

I would be bold enough to take away the 'maybe', and to say that what is 'yet to come' are all the key things that are wrapped up in the disciples' spiritual well-being and their acceptance before God. It includes the death of the Saviour for them the following day, his resurrection as the mark of God's acceptance of all that he did, his ascension back to glory opening the way for them, and his coming again in glory to wind up world history. It is possible to put together both Calvin's and Stott's understandings of this text.

J. Ramsey Michaels also has a helpful comment:

'The teaching ministry of the Holy Spirit builds on and develops the teaching ministry of Jesus himself. By making explicit what in Jesus' historical teaching was only implicit, the Spirit will prepare the disciples to face new enemies and seize new opportunities to extend Jesus' mission in the world. The implication is that the Spirit has done so precisely in this Gospel and in these last discourses.'[6]

In other words the Spirit would take the key things that were yet to come and teach them and apply them in such a way that the disciples would see more clearly the gospel and the mission that the Lord had for them in carrying his truth into a lost world.

---

5. John R. W. Stott, *Christ the Liberator*, Hodder and Stoughton, 1972, p.46.

6. J Ramsey Michaels, *New International Biblical Commentary on John*, Hendriksen/Paternoster, 1995, p. 284.

Will Jesus reveal new truths in the future history of the church?

I have heard incredible conclusions drawn from verse 12: 'I have much more to say to you, more than you can now bear.' I have heard it used to defend the idea that there are new truths which have no scriptural basis, which the disciples could not bear then, but which disciples down the years have legitimately discovered. I have also heard others say there are new key truths that the Spirit of God is now putting into people's minds which had not, up until that point, been revealed.

But what does Jesus mean? Is it that there would be new truths which would have no basis in his words and deeds? I don't believe that is the case. Rather with Leon Morris[7] I think the verse refers to the implications of the teaching of Jesus, the full understanding of what he came to do, and the application of those key saving events to hearts and lives by the Holy Spirit. In other words, there are *implications* of what Jesus is saying here, and there are *applications* of what is going to happen in the next few days which the Holy Spirit is going to take and apply to their lives when the time is right (when they are on the other side of Easter). Because 'he will bring glory to me [Jesus] by taking from what is mine' (16:14). It is not as if he is going to bring new truths that have no direct connection with the words and works of Jesus. The Holy Spirit will bring glory to Jesus after his death and resurrection by explaining to the disciples what they were not able to understand clearly in the Upper Room.

---

7. 'His ministry is built upon and is the necessary sequel to that of Christ', Leon Morris, *The Gospel According to John*, Marshall, Morgan and Scott, 1972, p. 701.

Also note, this is a *particular* promise to the apostles. But in a secondary sense, the Holy Spirit works in the same way in all believers. We do not have a promise to be guided into *all* truth in the particular way in which the apostles were enabled to write the true and trustworthy record and interpretation of the life and teachings, death and resurrection of the Lord Jesus, which would be the foundation for the church in every generation. But the Holy Spirit, the Spirit of Truth, is our guide to lead us in the direction of truth, to lead us into truth. And he does that by taking what belongs to Jesus and glorifying him by making it known to us.

The little phrase at the end of verse 13, 'He will tell you what is yet to come' could be translated: 'He will preach up what is yet to come.' In other words, he would proclaim to them the significance of the saving events that were yet to take place. For us that means he will bring us back to the truth testified to by the apostles – the apostolic witness to the revelation of God in Christ (i.e. the New Testament). Indeed he will bring us back to all Scripture (Old and New Testaments) and he will constantly want to magnify the Lord Jesus. He will be always guiding us away from dangers, pitfalls, sidetracks, wrong views, wrong ideas, errors and folly and bringing us back to the Lord Jesus Christ and the truth of his Word. He will always be doing that as our Guide. He is the Spirit of Truth who is concerned that the truth about Jesus will come out.

The marvellous last Gift
In all that Jesus has taught about the work of the Holy Spirit, we can see that there is no regeneration, there is no conviction of sin, there is no understanding of the gospel

of righteousness in Christ alone, there is no deliverance from judgment, apart from the convicting work of the Spirit. None of us would be Christians apart from his glorious, Jesus-magnifying work. He is our Advocate, he is the Counsel for the Defence who will stand by us and be with us. He is the invisible presence of Jesus, never to leave us or forsake us. He is the Spirit of truth, to show us the truth about ourselves and to bring us constantly to the feet of the One who is the truth. He is our Teacher who always wants to magnify Christ and to teach us the Word of God, which he inspired. He is the bringer of the peace of Christ. He is the One who takes all that Jesus has won for us on the Cross and seeks to apply it in our hearts and lives day by day, so that we might live in the light and glory of it, and delight in it. He is our Guide who will constantly lead us back to Jesus.

The presence of the Spirit is the gracious provision of Jesus for his disciples living as his followers in the real world. Would they be able to fulfil his command to testify to him as their Saviour? The Holy Spirit would help them. Would their message have an impact? The Holy Spirit would use it to the conviction and conversion of people. Would they remember and teach faithfully all that Jesus said and did? Would their 'foundation testimony' be true and reliable? The Holy Spirit would see to it!

Let me end this chapter with a quote from John Stott: 'The work of the Spirit can never be considered apart from Jesus Christ. He is the Spirit of Christ. His paramount concern is to reveal Christ to us and to form Christ in us.'[8]

---

8. John R. W. Stott, *Christ the Liberator*, Hodder and Stoughton, 1972, p.46.

He wants us to be ever trusting, loving and obeying Jesus. What a marvellous, wonderful, delightful, invigorating, life-giving, Jesus-glorifying, helpful last gift Jesus gave, in love, to his disciples! May we revel in the Spirit's ministry and not resist his prompting nor quench his activity in us. And to Jesus, the One he delights to glorify, be all the glory and the praise.

SECTION 4

Last Perspectives

Chapter 11

The Last Warning
(John 15:1-17)

There is an ongoing debate among commentators as to where the conversation beginning in John 15 took place. Let me explain. At the end of John 14 Jesus says, 'Come now; let us leave.' But did they actually leave or not? Was it rather like a pleasant evening with some friends, who though intending to leave at eleven o'clock, actually lasted until long after midnight! It is, however, possible that they did actually leave.

At the entrance to the Temple, on the way into the Sanctuary, was a big golden vine. The vine was one of the national symbols of the people of Israel. It is a significant biblical symbol that is used to describe the people of God in Ezekiel 15, 17, 19, and in the Maccabean period it was found on coins. So maybe Jesus saw the golden vine and used it as a prompt or visual aid for the disciples for what he wanted to say to them. If so, and personally I think this is likely, it would mean that the conversation recorded in John 15 occurred on the way to Gethsemane.

Be that as it may, the power of what Jesus is saying in verse 1 would not have been lost on the disciples. Jesus is the *true* vine in contrast to Israel who was the professing vine. What Jesus means is clear and startling. Israel was supposed to be the obedient people of God, but faithful Israel had narrowed down to just one person – Jesus

'I am the true vine, and my Father is the gardener. [2]He cuts off every branch in me that bears no fruit, while every branch that does bear fruit he trims clean so that it will be even more fruitful. [3]You are already clean because of the word I have spoken to you. [4]Remain in me, and I will remain in you. No branch can bear fruit by itself; it must remain in the vine. Neither can you bear fruit unless you remain in me.

'[5]I am the vine; you are the branches. If a man remains in me and I in him, he will bear much fruit; apart from me you can do nothing. [6]If anyone does not remain in me, he is like a branch that is thrown away and withers; such branches are picked up, thrown into the fire and burned. [7]If you remain in me and my words remain in you, ask whatever you wish, and it will be given you. [8]This is to my Father's glory, that you bear much fruit, showing yourselves to be my disciples.

'[9]As the Father has loved me, so have I loved you. Now remain in my love. [10]If you obey my commands, you will remain in my love, just as I have obeyed my Father's commands and remain in his love. [11]I have told you this so that my joy may be in you and that your joy may be complete. [12]My command is this: Love each other as I have loved you. [13]Greater love has no-one than this, that he lay down his life for his friends. [14]You are my friends if you do what I command. [15]I no longer call you servants, because a servant does not know his master's business. Instead, I have called you friends, for everything that I learned from my Father I have made known to you. [16]You did not choose me, but I chose you and appointed you to go and bear fruit – fruit that will last. Then the Father will give you whatever you ask in my name. [17]This is my command: Love each other' (John 15:1-17).

himself! He alone is the One who perfectly kept his Father's commands (14:31). He is the only true Israelite! Israel had traded on her spiritual past, and was in desperate need of the work of 'the Gardener'. Israel needed to return to God for emergency care.

In my mother's house we had a vine in a greenhouse. Every year we hoped for fruit and every year we were disappointed. What fruit the vine produced was hard, tiny and bitter. We talked to it, put fertilizer on it, pruned it and did what we could to improve it – all to no avail! The trouble was we were not expert gardeners.

This was just like what was happening to Israel. They appeared to promise much but never delivered. They were a fruitless vine that was proving useless, and in desperate need of the Gardener. They required a vital relationship with God's Son who is the life-source of the New Covenant people of God. For Jesus made it plain that he is the vine and that his disciples are the branches (15:5). There is no fruit and there is no life apart from him. Fruit is the evidence of life, and where there is regularly no fruit we rightly deduce there is no life.

What does Jesus mean in verses 2 and 6? Whenever I have preached or taught from this passage, I have always been asked this question: 'Is it possible to be saved and then subsequently lost, as would at first appear on a superficial reading of these verses?'

Jesus is thinking here in verses 2 and 6 about those who *profess* to be people of God (like the Jews) or profess to be followers of him (like Judas), but who are not real believers – and probably Judas is especially in mind. It is not good enough to be around Jesus or claim to follow him, unless there is a real grafting into him by faith.

Belonging to the professing church, being 'around' Jesus, or even being at special blessed moments (like John 13), or working for the Lord (as Judas had) don't make us *his*. I love the comment of Martin Luther that the ability to use 'personal pronouns' is of the essence of New Testament Christianity. Luther said many could say Jesus is the Saviour of the world, but only the true Christian could describe him as 'my Saviour' and 'my Lord'!

Here is a warning by Jesus against mere profession, and fruitless lives. Fruitfulness is the evidence of life (15:8). There is a stark contrast here between fruitful Christians and lost unbelievers. There is no middle ground. Let us be sure that by faith we are in vital personal union with Jesus the Vine as our Saviour, the One in whom alone there is life.

Fruit, in the sense that Jesus means, is what shows us to be disciples of Jesus. It is the evidence of life and spiritual health. It is not that we work to become his disciples, but that when grafted into him by faith his life flows through us as we abide in him and produce 'fruit'. I like the comment of John Stott: 'Thus the Christian is likened to a fruit tree, not a Christmas tree. For the fruit grows on a fruit tree whereas the decorations are only tied on to a Christmas tree.'[1] Fruit shows the real disciples of Jesus (15:8). Reality is seen by evidence, not just claims.

But what is the fruit? To quote John Stott again: 'In fact I do not hesitate to say that fruitfulness means Christlikeness.'[2] Undoubtedly this is the basis of it all. The fruit of the Spirit, as described in Galatians 5:22-23, is Christlike character being formed in some measure by

1. John R W Stott, *Christ the Liberator*, p.55.
2. *ibid* p.52.

the Spirit of God in every true believer.

Unless we show that we have been with Christ and display something of him to the world around us, they will not believe our words. Much harm has been done by words not backed up by godly living. But though this is the basis of it all, I think it means more. It means '*every* demonstration of vitality of faith, to which according to verses 9-17 reciprocal love above all belongs.'[3] Fruitful Christian living will be seen in loving relationships with other Christians: 'by this all men will know you are my disciples if you love one another' (John 13:35). Bad relationships amongst believers have done much harm to the cause of the gospel.

Again, although this is undoubtedly true I think it means still more than 'every vitality of faith'. In verse 16 there is an echo, which the disciples would later have understood clearly, of the great commission 'to *go* and make disciples of all nations'. There is clearly a missionary element to the 'fruit' in verse 16.

In addition, they have been chosen by God's sovereign choice to produce 'fruit that will last'. What more lasting fruit is there than to be the link in the chain of someone's conversion, so that they come to know Christ for themselves and spend eternity in 'the Father's house' in heaven. That is eternally lasting fruit!

So the fruit that Jesus wants to see in his disciples, that is the evidence of real life in him, is some measure of his character being formed in us, and of us being influential in a lost world for him. Much of this fruit may be better observed by others, and this side of eternity we may not

---

3. G. Beasley Murray, *John*, Word Bible Commentary, 1987, p.273, italics mine.

know those for whom we have been a 'link in the chain'. But we should certainly want to be fruitful in all the senses mentioned above, and indeed that desire is an evidence of real life!

It is worth recording here that Jesus tells the disciples that they are indeed clean (15:3); they have listened and obeyed his gospel summons, and they will thus be pruned by the expert Gardener (the Father) to produce more fruit (15:2). Pruning may not be pleasant for a plant (if it had feelings) but it delivers the fruit! The disciples will experience some hard pruning, but they are in the safe hands of the Father whose skill will produce the fruit they have been chosen to produce (15:16).

Malcolm Muggeridge has put it like this: 'Supposing you eliminated suffering, what a dreadful place the world would be! I would almost rather eliminate happiness. The world would be the most ghastly place because everything that corrects the tendency of this unspeakable little creature, man, to feel over-important would disappear. He's bad enough now but he would be absolutely intolerable if he never suffered.'[4]

I have also been told that C. H. Spurgeon suffered from bad health in the latter part of his ministry and found this to be something that cast him back on God and improved his preaching.

Joni Eareckson Tada's famous comment bears repetition: 'God could have healed me, but he did a greater miracle, he left me in a wheelchair and put a smile on my face.'

How then are we to live fruitful lives? That will be every true Christian's greatest desire. The key warning,

4. Malcolm Muggeridge, *Jesus Rediscovered*, Fontana, 1969.

and indeed the key point of the passage, comes in verse 5:
'If a man remains in me and I in him, he will bear much
fruit; *apart from me you can do nothing*.' If we are to live
for Christ and be fruitful disciples we need above all to
learn this secret. It would make a great motto for every
Christian noticeboard, and it would be hard to think of a
better church motto! Nothing can be accomplished *for*
him, apart from him and his life-giving strength.

Work, even Christian work, can so often be done in our
own strength with God's blessing being sought afterwards. We need to understand that this is fruitless work.

Jesus calls us to 'remain' or 'abide' in him (15:4) and
to abide in his love (15:9). It is very important to grasp that
abiding in him is the only way to live fruitful Christian
lives. In the next three sections I want us to look at what
'abiding in Jesus' means.

1. Abiding in Jesus means taking his Word seriously
Remaining in Jesus is connected with letting his words
remain or abide in us (15:7). It is more than being merely
'hearers of the Word', it means being 'doers of it' (15:10).
Obedience to the Word of God is the way of fruitfulness
and the way to abide in Christ.

When I was a young Christian, being somewhat bewildered by the amount of new information I was getting, I
asked an older Christian to explain to me the key ingredi-
ent in Christian living. He said 'obedience is the key to
Christian living'! I thought that was too easy an answer
and said so, but the more I have lived as a believer the
more I realise it was a profound answer. When we
understand how much God loves us, enough to send his
own Son to die for us, when we see that love so displayed

in the selfless love of Jesus, how can we possibly think that it is in our best interests to be disobedient? God knows us best, and surely we will want to know and do those things that please the One who loved us so?

Jesus makes plain here, too, that obedience is the way of joy for the Christian (15:11, see Chapter 14, *Christian Joy*). There is nobody more miserable than a disobedient Christian!

The key command that Jesus singles out here as a kind of test of all other commands by its outworking, is spelled out in verses 12 and 17. The disciples are to love one another as he loves them. Unselfish love in putting others first will show that we have been touched by the unselfish love of Calvary, and will help us convince a lost world that there is an alternative to self-centred living in following Jesus.

So we need to take the Word of God seriously and seek to obey it in practice.

2. Abiding in Jesus means dependence on Christ for everything

Fruitful Christians acknowledge that they cannot *understand* his words or *obey* his commands without his help and his life infilling them and enabling them so to do. Unless his life pulsates through us we will not be fruitful.

That dependence is best expressed in prayer, for that shows *par excellence* our *need of* and *dependence* on God. When my son, who is eight, asked me for a bike for Christmas, he was saying that unless I helped him he would be unable to gain what he wanted by his own resources. When we pray we express our gratitude to and dependence on God our heavenly Father for everything.

Prayer is one of the great emphases of these chapters: 'Ask me for anything in my name, and I will do it' (John 14:14); 'Remain in my words' and 'ask whatever you wish, and it will be given you' (John 15:7). This kind of prayer wants what Jesus wants, and it wants to be obedient. Desire the Father's purpose for you – to be fruitful – and 'then the Father will give whatever you ask in my name' (15:16).

Unless we pray we will not bear fruit.

3. Abiding in Jesus means remaining and abiding in his love

I like the superb comment of G. Beasley Murray: 'This must mean *primarily* remaining in the love that Jesus has for his disciples – rejoicing in its reality, depending on its support, doing nothing to grieve it, but on the contrary engaging in that which delights the Lover.'[5]

'Remaining in his love' means basking in the wonderful love of Calvary day in and day out. As Christians we can never safely move far away from the foot of the Cross, for there we see the wonder of the love of Christ for us. Has that become over-familiar to you, Christian? An old Christian once said to me, 'Grace should always bring a tear of joy to our eyes.' Maybe we need to ask the Lord to enable us to bask more in his love, that he might rekindle in our hearts that sense of wonder at his love that leads to obedience to him.

His love for us, the joy of it and our gratitude for it, should touch our *hearts* by bringing us to prayer and praise, thus expressing our joyful dependence on the One who from eternity planned to take us to spend eternity

---

5. G. Beasley Murray, *John*, p.273, italics mine.

with him. It should touch our *wills* to obey his truth,
understanding he has our best interests at heart, and that
obedience to him is the way of joy. It should touch our
minds to seek to know and understand his will for us from
his Word, so that we might obey it. To do that, we humbly
need to get to know his Word, the Bible, better.

Let us see how these things are brought out in six key
points in verses 9-16.

(1) *They are to rejoice in his love and remain in it* (15:9).
The other side of Calvary would reveal more fully the
enormity of his love for them.

(2) *They are to take joy and find joy in obedience to his
wishes* (15:10-11). So saying, we need to take preaching
seriously and to study the Scriptures with other Christians, as well as on our own.

(3) *They are to delight in his friendship* (15:13-15). What
is the essential difference between a servant and a friend?
You may never know what your boss is thinking. These
days you may, sadly, never know till you are handed a
brown envelope and told you are redundant! But a friend
has access to the thinking, plans and desires of his friend
who enjoys sharing these things with him. Friendship
with God means God *taking us into his confidence*
because he views us as his friends! It is a wonderful
privilege for disciples of the King of kings to be described
as his friends, and the greatness of the privilege should
bring us much joy!

(4) *They are to see the church as a meeting of friends
called to love each other, because each is precious to the*

Lord (15:14, 15). Why is fellowship in some churches less than in a golf club? There is nothing greater than the fellowship and friendship of real believers. We should value the church, because Jesus values his friends.

(5) *They are to be secure in his choice of them* (15:16). Not every Christian knows exactly when he was converted, but he will know there was a time when he crossed from 'death to life'. But behind his choice is the greater truth that the Lord has chosen all his disciples. Each disciple can look back and see God's hand drawing him in love to Jesus.

The disciples, troubled and insecure as they were, could never have security in Jesus if their eternal well-being depended on their decision. Neither could we! If it depended on me I might be lost tomorrow! But behind our decision to follow Christ is the sovereign decision of our Saviour to choose us, and we can be secure that he knows his sheep, they are safe in his hand, and 'they shall never perish' (John 10:28).

The doctrine of election is not for idle speculation but for encouragement and praise to God. It gives a sense of security to a believer. The disciples were chosen for a purpose, 'to go and bear fruit', and disciples today have been given God's grace for exactly the same reason.

(6) *They needed to remember that Jesus had a task for them* (15:16). When despondent and feeling worthless they needed to know they were loved and had work to do for the Lord.

Conclusion

This section then is about the crucial importance of
abiding/remaining in Christ. It is about the folly of trying
to be fruitful Christians apart from a continual dependence on Christ. The branches will be fruitless without
dependence on the vine. This key section comes as a last
crucial warning from the lips of Jesus: 'Apart from me
you can do nothing.'

Let me sum up what abiding/remaining in Christ
means by using a statement of J. C. Ryle: 'Abide in me.
Cling to me. Stick fast to me. Live the life of close and
intimate communion with me. Get nearer and nearer to
me. Roll every burden on me. Cast your whole weight on
me. Never let go your hold on me for a moment.'[6]

How right he is!

---

6. J. C. Ryle, *Expository Thoughts on the Gospels*, p. 335.

12

Living in the Real World
(John 15:18-27; 16:1-4, 17-33)

Jesus was dealing with disciples who were troubled, confused and afraid. Jesus' first comfort for the troubled disciples was to focus their attention on heaven. He was going to leave them, he was going to death, in order that the way for heaven might be opened up for them. Jesus said then, and says to us now, that if we have troubled hearts we need to focus on what he actually came to do. The final outcome of what he came to do for his children is a place in his Father's house, being with him there in his presence forever.

But what about the intervening period between the time that he would leave the disciples and the time that they would arrive in the Father's house? His second comfort was his promise to send 'another Counsellor' who, in terms of ministry and presence, would be to them all that Jesus had been to them. The Holy Spirit, instead of just being *with* them, would be *in* them.

The disciples felt like orphans because the heart of their trouble was that Jesus was leaving them. Jesus therefore informed them that he was going away to accomplish their eternal redemption. They would see him again after he rose from the dead, and because he was alive they too would live. He would then send the Holy Spirit to enable them to obey him and live for him. The

Holy Spirit would also be the means of Jesus coming to them and manifesting himself to them. In fact, the Father, Jesus and the Spirit – the Trinity – would manifest themselves to them. So Jesus would still be with them by the Spirit, the One whom he called 'another Counsellor'.

But another reason why they felt troubled and distressed was the thought of facing the challenges of the world in the absence of Jesus. They faced the danger of having their faith shaken in the difficult days that lay ahead when Jesus was no longer with them. It was the challenges of living in the real world without the Lord Jesus that was deepening the crisis for the disciples.

Jesus had told them by way of encouragement that he would send the Holy Spirit to them. Nevertheless Jesus knew that his disciples needed instruction about what it would mean to live as his followers in the real world. It is on this issue that he focused his teaching in John 15 and 16.

Take, for example, what he says in 16:1-4: 'All this I have told you so that you will not go astray. ... I have told you this, so that when the time comes you will remember that I warned you. I did not tell you this at first because I was with you.' Jesus told them what would happen to them, so that when it did happen they would not be so taken by surprise that their faith would be shaken unduly. He wanted them to face realistically and honestly the toughness of living in a world in rebellion against him.

I am going to give a quick overview of John 15:1-16:16 because I want you to see what was going on in the Upper Room. There are three sections in this one block of material from 15:1 to 16:16. In these sections there is a very important movement to which I want to draw your attention before going on to look in detail at 15:18-27.

In 15:1-17, as we saw in the previous chapter, Jesus was talking to the disciples about fruitful Christian living. He told them about a very important truth; in fact there is no more important truth for Christians to learn: 'Apart from me you can do nothing' (verse 5). Jesus was warning the disciples that if they wanted to live fruitful lives for God, as indeed God intended (for they had been chosen to produce fruit that would last), then they needed to abide in him. They could not live the Christian life, except by being in continual contact with their Saviour.

The end of this section is very hopeful (verse 16). The disciples were being encouraged by Jesus to go into the world and there to live fruitful lives, lives that would win other people for Christ. But he also reminds them that behind their choice of him was his choice of them. Verse 16 is a verse I always share with every person that I meet who has just become a Christian. I say, 'When you made a decision to follow Christ you did make a choice. But I want to tell you something wonderful. Behind your choice was God's choice of you. Now think back, hasn't God been at work in your life to bring you to this moment of decision?' Each one has instantly replied 'yes'. God has been at work.

So the first seventeen verses of John 15 are very optimistic. But the note changes from verses 18-27, a section that carries on in 16:1-4. In 18-27 Jesus spells out what it means to live in the real world. True, they will see other people won for their Master. Yet Jesus warned them that when they would go into the real world and live for him it would not be a bed of roses. It was not going to be a Billy Graham crusade every week. They were not necessarily going to see crowds of people becoming Christians. Although there would be lasting fruit, it was going to be tough out there. They were going to feel the pressure of living as Jesus' guerillas in a world in rebellion against him, and they needed to be prepared. Jesus told them what was going to happen because he wanted them to go into the hostile world with their eyes opened.

Then we come to the third block of material which contains teaching about the Holy Spirit (15:26, 27; 16:5-16). Jesus wanted them to understand the equipment, the Holy Spirit, he was going to give them, so that they would be able to live for him and their faith remain unshaken.

1. Disciples and the secular world (15:18-27)

Firstly, in 15:18 Jesus said to the disciples, 'If the world hates you, keep in mind that it hated me first.' What they needed to understand was whose side they were on. It can be very hard to live for Christ as part of a small minority. We all like to be popular. It can be very difficult when we find that other people do not like what we stand for (though nothing like as difficult as it is for Christians elsewhere in the world). Nevertheless Christians in our society can be marginalised and ostracised, sometimes in not so polite ways. In such situations, we are to remember who it is we are lining up behind – the Son of God!

Secondly, Jesus continued in verse 19: 'If you belonged to the world, it would love you as its own. As it is, you do not belong to the world, but I have chosen you out of the world.' The 'world' is the term Jesus used to describe the whole of the human race in rebellion against God. The world according to the teaching of Jesus is doomed. It is going to perish. This teaching is found in the

'If the world hates you, keep in mind that it hated me first. [19]If you belonged to the world, it would love you as its own. As it is, you do not belong to the world, but I have chosen you out of the world. That is why the world hates you. [20]Remember the words I spoke to you: "No servant is greater than his master." If they persecuted me, they will persecute you also. If they obeyed my teaching, they will obey yours also. [21]They will treat you this way because of my name, for they do not know the One who sent me. [22]If I had not come and spoken to them, they would not be guilty of sin. Now, however, they have no excuse for their sin. [23]He who hates me hates my Father as well. [24]If I had not done among them what no-one else did, they would not be guilty of sin. But now they have seen these miracles, and yet they have hated both me and my Father. [25]But this is to fulfil what is written in their Law: "They hated me without reason."

[26]'When the Counsellor comes, whom I will send to you from the Father, the Spirit of truth who goes out from the Father, he will testify about me; [27]but you also must testify, for you have been with me from the beginning' (John 15:18-27).

most famous verse in the New Testament: 'For God so loved the world that he gave his one and only Son that whoever believes in him shall not *perish* but have eternal life' (John 3:16). 'If the world hates you,' says Jesus, 'remember the world and all its rebellion is doomed. It is going to face my judgement. But you don't belong to a doomed world; your real home is in my Father's house.' Or as the Lord revealed to John in the book of Revelation: they belong not in the old world that is to be judged, but they belong in the 'new heavens and the new earth'.

Jesus has chosen us out of the world. Isn't that great news? We have been chosen to a different destiny altogether. In the pressure of living in the real world, remember that!

Thirdly, Jesus said in verse 20: 'No servant is greater than his master.' The same phrase occurs in John 13:16: 'I tell you the truth, no servant is greater than his master nor is a messenger greater than the one who sent him.' There Jesus used that pithy little saying to remind the disciples that he has given them an example of how he wants them to live. In that sense no servant is greater than his master; the servant should live the way his master lives. But in 15:20 the saying is used differently to remind us that if Jesus was given a certain kind of treatment we should not expect anything different.

Jesus doesn't want his disciples to be naïve. If the world wanted to eradicate Jesus and get rid of him, and plotted to crucify him, don't be surprised when the world wants to push us aside because we are little reflections of the Light of the world.

Have you noticed the way the popular press handles its idols? As soon as there is any ground for criticism it will

be magnified because human nature likes to pull down
idols. You know the old comment about the new Vicar:
'the first year they idolised, the second year they criticised, the third year they scandalised and the fourth year
they ostracised.' It is the human heart, isn't it!

Although he was the Light of the world, Jesus was
crucified, because as the Truth of God he was too uncomfortable to have around. The world wanted to be rid of
Jesus, so do not be surprised if the world sometimes wants
to push us out of the way.

Verses 21 and 23 go together: 'They will treat you this
way because of my name, for they do not know the One
who sent me' (15:21). 'He who hates me hates my Father
as well' (15:23). Don Carson comments: 'Every attitude
directed towards him is no less directed towards God.
This 'profound Christology .... accounts for the persecution Jesus' followers will face'.[1] Jesus is saying here very
clearly that a person cannot disregard Jesus and claim to
know God.

Fourthly, in verses 22 and 24 (a set of verses that go
together like 21 and 23) Jesus informed his disciples that
his coming has heightened the individual responsibility
of those who have seen or heard about him: 'If I had not
come and spoken to them they would not be guilty of sin.
Now, however, they have no excuse for their sin' (15:22);
'If I had not done among them what no-one else did they
would not be guilty of sin' (15:24).

Jesus did not mean that they would not be guilty
sinners if he had not come. What he was stressing was that
now they are guilty of the heart of sin which is unbelief in
him: 'When [the Spirit] comes, he will convict the world

---

1. D. A. Carson, *Gospel According to John*, IVP, 1991, page 527.

of guilt in regard to sin and righteousness and judgment: in regard to sin, because men do not believe in me' (16:8, 9).

If you stopped a person in the street and asked him, What do Christians believe is the heart of sin?, you would probably get an answer like 'adultery'. But according to the New Testament, the heart of sin is unbelief. In the light of Jesus' words and works, rejection of him is very serious. It is the very heart of the sinful rebellion of the arrogant human heart against its Maker. 'Rejection of Jesus' words and works is thus the rejection of the clearest light, the fullest revelation and therefore it incurs the most central, deep-stained guilt.'[2]

Fifthly, Jesus could look back on his life and, with honesty, truthfulness and humility, say that he was hated without a reason: 'But now they have seen these miracles, and yet they have hated both me and my Father. But this is to fulfil what is written in their Law: "They hated me without reason" ' (15:24-25). If we are hated, we need to be very careful that we are hated 'without a reason'. I remember someone saying to me that he had a lot of problems at work, which he had assumed occurred because he was a Christian. But I had found this particular individual to be very difficult, somewhat awkward and angular, uptight as well as being 'upright'. Maybe it was because of his awkwardness and his nit-picking, negative nature that people found him difficult to work with. We need to be very careful that the ground of the accusation against us is because we reflect Jesus.

In a previous parish in which I served I was the second evangelical minister in 700 years! My first two years were

2. D.A. Carson, *Gospel According to John*, IVP, 1991, page 526.

quite difficult. I had been there for about six months when someone came to see me. He said to me, 'If you go on preaching like this you will have no congregation and no choir!' It was a church with some choral tradition. For a moment, the whole of my life flashed before my eyes. I thought this is the first charge I have had on my own as a minister, and I am going to blow it! After only six months here, the place is going to fall apart! Then I caught myself and I said to him, 'My friend, if there is something in me that has caused offence to you I am deeply and truly sorry. If you have found something in your new vicar that has made things difficult for you personally, I apologise unreservedly. But if your trouble is with my message, if your trouble is with the Word of God and what I preach, your problem is not with me, it is with the Lord, and the sooner you fix it with him the better for you eternally.'

I went home and talked to my wife and we prayed about it. After that, in the pulpit I determined to be as clear and forthright as I could be in preaching the truth in love. Outside the pulpit I determined to be as gentle as God would enable me to be in terms of personal dealings with people. Happily, the church doubled in size. But it didn't look like that would happen at that moment in time!

We need to be careful that the ground of offence is our Lord and not us. We need to make sure there isn't a just reason to accuse us.

Sixthly, when living in the real world we need to remember that Jesus knows all about it (16:4). His knowledge is more than mere information about the situation. A good example of this is when the Israelites cried out to God in the misery of their suffering in Egypt. God said in response, 'I remember my covenant. I know what you are going through.' When God says 'I know' he means not only 'I know what is going to happen' but also 'I am providing for my people'. Jesus knew the challenges facing the disciples, and he wanted them to know that he would provide for them in those difficult situations.

Jesus took the time to educate the disciples for living in the real world. When his attention could have been focused on the agony awaiting him on the Cross the following day, his concern was not for himself but for his disciples. What love Jesus showed in carefully preparing the disciples for what lay ahead. Jesus informed his disciples that he knew what it was like to live in the real world.

The Saviour will do all that is necessary to settle troubled hearts amongst his disciples today. So we are not to be shaken by living in the real world. Don't let it compromise our faith. By paying careful attention to the teaching of the One who spoke, and still speaks, from his Word to his disciples, we can abide in Jesus and be fruitful disciples.

2. Disciples and ecclesiastical opposition (16:1-4)

It isn't just opposition from the world at large that poses a problem for us as Christians and causes our faith to be challenged and sometimes shaken. Difficulties can come from ecclesiastical opposition, opposition from within the professing church.

The professing church of the disciples' day was the Jewish Church. Although it was suffering under the Roman imperial occupation, it was extremely powerful and very influential. It was numerically very strong, numbering approximately all of the nation of Israel. It was looking for the coming of the Messiah and was largely concerned about the keeping of God's law.

Yet the truth about the Jewish Church at that time was that, despite the fact that they were in theory awaiting the Messiah, they resisted Jesus when he came as God's anointed messenger. It was with heavy irony that Jesus said in John 15:25: 'But this is to fulfil what is written in *their* law.' The law belonged to God, and yet it was something that they claimed belonged to them. But it had become theirs in the sense that it had been disconnected, in their minds, from loving God and serving him. In fact, the Old Testament condemned them, as Jesus proved when he said that they fulfilled the prophecy, 'They hated me without a cause' (Psalm 69:4 and John 15:25). The word 'their' also points to the fact that instead of them submitting to God's law and seeing the signs of the fulfilment of God's promises in the coming of his Messiah, they were missing the whole point of the law in their own religiosity and their own self-righteousness.

There is a very interesting comment by Jesus at the close of 16:3 that is so easily missed if it is not read carefully and in context: 'They will put you out of the synagogue; in fact a time is coming when anyone who

'All this I have told you so that you will not go astray. [2]They will put you out of the synagogue; in fact, a time is coming when anyone who kills you will think he is offering a service to God. [3]They will do such things because they have not known the Father or me. [4]I have told you this, so that when the time comes you will remember that I warned you. I did not tell you this at first because I was with you' (John 16:1-4).

kills you will think he is offering a service to God. They will do such things because they have not known the Father or me.' F. F. Bruce notes that the last phrase can be more helpfully translated as 'they have not come to know the Father or me'.[3] They had plenty of opportunities to come to know God, indeed their very existence as a people was because of God's goodness to them. They had the privilege of God's law and yet they had not availed themselves of it to help them serve God.

Look back to 15:21: 'They will treat you this way because of my name, for they do not know the One who sent me.' Jesus was actually telling the disciples that the then professing church was just like the world, for it did not know God through his Son. The only way to know God is through acceptance of his Son, but the professing church had resisted the Son. In doing so, it had become like the world; in fact the world was in the church. That was one of the reasons why Jesus said to the disciples: 'All this I have told you so that you will not go astray' (16:1). They were to understand that he was still in control and working out his purposes even when there was opposition from the professing church.

What damage is done by newspaper reports of how the church appears not to believe what it should believe. What time is lost in witnessing when we have to explain why the church, which should be honouring the name of Christ and loving his Word, has somehow 'lost it' in a whole kind of mass of religious practice and observance! I can remember somebody in my previous parish whose big obstacle to becoming a Christian was the Resurrection. I prayed often for him and spent a lot of time with

3. F. F. Bruce, *John*, Eerdmans, 1992, p. 317.

him. I can still remember the occasion when he actually said to me, with some force, 'Now that one of your bishops denies what I have always had trouble with, you can take the pressure off me! I don't have to believe it any more than he does.' Although I was saddened by his words, I responded, 'Oh no! You are both in the same category of opposing Christ.'

I want to draw some parallels with the church today which we shouldn't miss. Of course, the Jewish Church is not an exact parallel with the Christian Church, but there is a close connection between them that makes possible some interesting and very important comparisons.

First of all, there can be *resistance in the professing church of Christ today to taking Christ and his Word seriously*. Theological liberalism has infected the church: 'You can't believe all that Jesus is said to have done. Surely there must be "this" or "that" qualification for today's world.' Often there is particular resistance to the uniqueness and finality of Jesus as the only way to know God. Jesus himself highlighted this resistance in the Jewish church: 'They will treat you this way because of my name, for they do not know the One who sent me' (15:21); 'He who hates me hates my Father as well' (15:23).

Recently I met a number of folk who wanted to be involved in lay ministry of the Word in their denomination. I asked each of them this question: 'Do you believe Jesus is the only way to God or do you believe that Jesus is the best way of all the alternatives?' All replied, 'I believe that Jesus is the best of all the alternatives, but not the only one of the alternatives.' That was resistance in the professing church today to the uniqueness of Jesus!

Let me recount another story. I don't want to depress

you, but we have to face reality. Once I went to a training conference with a very intensive programme. After the meal at the end of a very long day, I discussed with another minister his church situation. Trying to get the conversation on to more spiritual matters, I asked him, 'What are you doing for the Decade of Evangelism in your church?' He replied, 'Absolutely nothing! I am hugely embarrassed about it all.' I then asked him, 'Why are you embarrassed?' His reply was, 'Because I don't really agree with it.' I then said, 'Well, don't you think that Christ is at least the best of all the alternatives?' (I would want to say a lot more, for he is the only way to God.) He responded, 'Oh no! Not at all. I don't even think he is the best! I actually only happen to be involved in the church because I was brought up in England. If I had been brought up somewhere else, such as India, it would have been different. I actually would have preferred to have been brought up there because I think Eastern mysticism is a better way.' I was so gobsmacked it took me some while to regain my equilibrium! Please don't think that all or even many ministers are like that!

But sometimes we will find extraordinary opposition to Christ and his truth within the professing church. Resistance to taking Christ seriously, resistance to the uniqueness of Jesus, resistance to a personal knowledge of Jesus. I have been to church conferences where, frankly, it would have been embarrassing for some of the delegates to talk about knowing Christ and having a personal walk with him. It was much easier for them to discuss a new ecclesiastical bill that was coming before the church, or to speak together about an organ or a new roof or redecoration, anything as long as they did not have to talk about a personal relationship with Jesus Christ!

Of course, many people have never been taught the uniqueness of Jesus. I have learned from serving in churches other than established evangelical churches, that sadly some congregations have never really had the opportunity to hear of Jesus as the only way to God. But there can be nonetheless real resistance to a personal knowledge of Jesus.

Once, when I was coming home on the train from a meeting, I couldn't help overhearing two people having an interesting conversation about going to church. I think they had been talking about the publishing of Christian poetry. The one with the loudest voice (I could hear every word he spoke) said, 'Oh yes, I go to church sometimes. I go sort of infrequently but I go kind of regularly. I go when I have a real need and I am really up against it. I know that is where I need to be when I am facing problems because I know that in the end I need to turn to God at those times. But when things are going better I wouldn't actually want to go to church too often because I wouldn't want to get fanatical about it!'

What an incredible misuse of the word *fanatical*! It isn't fanatical to want to treat the Lord of glory as the steering wheel of your life rather than as the spare wheel of your life, as a friend of mine used to put it. Some people have this mentality that God can be treated like a spare wheel. Bang! 'I have a problem, I wonder where God is and why he is not here to help.' They want God there for them on their terms, not on his. They want him in emergencies, but not as part of their lives. Extraordinary resistance to a personal knowledge of Jesus, to letting Christ get close.

It is also possible, in the professing church, for *religious practice or moral law to be substituted for a personal knowledge of Jesus Christ*. It is possible even to stand for biblical moral values because of one's family background, church upbringing or whatever, and to have no personal knowledge of Jesus Christ. That was what was happening among the Jews at the time when Jesus was on earth. They would have stood up for the moral law of God, but they were resistant to God's Messiah. And that can be possible in the church today.

We who want to take Jesus seriously and to rejoice in a personal knowledge of God, who want to honour his Word and are impatient of practices that distract from Jesus, can be marginalised *sometimes* by the professing church and even *opposed* by the professing church. That puts us under a lot of pressure and often shakes us.

But Jesus does not want us to be shaken when these things happen. How does Jesus want his disciples to react?

The first thing Jesus says by implication in 16:2 is, *Don't judge the professing church*. Don't leave it easily. Have you noticed that he says, '*They* will put you out of the synagogue.' The early believers did not leave the professing church of their time, they were thrown out of it. Let the church be the ones who put us out as we remain faithful to Jesus. The time may come for us to go, but don't leave easily, don't give up lightly on the professing church.

Secondly, let us not be shaken in our faith but go on standing for the truth. We are not to let our hearts be troubled, but instead we are to trust in the Father and in Jesus (John 14:1).

Thirdly, we are to make sure that we are *abiding in Christ*, and not just being evangelically religious, having a substitute religion for the real thing by going through the evangelical motions of religious practice. John Stott has referred to 'the tradition of the evangelical elders'. People can sometimes follow the tradition of belonging to an evangelical church and yet not be converted; they can be 'evangelically' religious and yet have no real knowledge of Jesus. Even real disciples of Jesus can get into a position of substituting religious practice for a knowledge of Christ and truly abiding in him. The evidence of real discipleship is bearing fruit, 'showing yourself to be my disciples' (15:18), and fruit is only produced as we abide in Christ. Abiding in Christ is very important. In the group of disciples there was a Judas. There was one who appeared to be very near to Jesus, but who was not.

Fourthly, although it is not directly mentioned by Jesus here, there is another response that we need to acknowledge. Let us recall the background against which these disciples were working. They were a very small minority. After three years of the ministry of Jesus there appeared to be only several hundred disciples[4], although soon there would be thousands! *There is always a tendency for real believers to underestimate the numbers that God will actually save.* Remember Elijah who thought that very few had refused to bow to Baal, when in reality God had 7,000 who faithfully worshipped him. When we read the New Testament we see the believers grew greatly in number. We, too, need to lift up our eyes and see what

---

4. 120 were gathered in Jerusalem (Acts 1:15, 16); 'more than 500' – probably in Galilee (1 Corinthians 15:6). See discussion on Acts 1:15 in *Acts* by F. F. Bruce, NICNT, Eerdmans, 1988.

God is doing in the world and in the church of our day, in terms of how many people the Lord is leading to himself, not just in our country but throughout the world. How encouraging!

We have seen with what care and love Jesus prepared the disciples for what lay ahead. How concerned he was to encourage them! How determined he was to tell them the truth, the way it really is in the world and the way it would be for them.

A last encouragement[5] (16:17-33).

Recently I have had to admit that I needed new spectacles. I found that if I looked down when I was preaching I could not always focus on my notes! That is not a prescription for clear and fluent preaching! I have ended up with 'varifocals', and they have taken a little getting used to! So I am conscious of the importance of focus at the moment!

Getting our focus right as Christians is very important, and not always easy. You remember we have already seen that the disciples were troubled, confused, and feeling like orphans. Chapter 16 begins with the description of disciples, under pressure and in danger of going astray, and we have seen Jesus' careful teaching to prevent that from happening. But in verse 6 we find they were still upset; upset at the prospect of the absence of Jesus, and of coping with the challenge of living in a hostile world without Jesus being physically with them (15:18ff.). All of this caused them to feel troubled.

What did they need in order to regain their balance?

5. You will find more on this section in Chapter 14, 'Christian Joy'.

Some of his disciples said to one another, 'What does he mean by saying, "In a little while you will see me no more, and then after a little while you will see me," and "Because I am going to the Father"?' [18]They kept asking, 'What does he mean by "a little while"? We don't understand what he is saying.'

[19]Jesus saw that they wanted to ask him about this, so he said to them, 'Are you asking one another what I meant when I said, "In a little while you will see me no more, and then after a little while you will see me"? [20]I tell you the truth, you will weep and mourn while the world rejoices. You will grieve, but your grief will turn to joy. [21]A woman giving birth to a child has pain because her time has come; but when her baby is born she forgets the anguish because of her joy that a child is born into the world. [22]So with you: Now is your time of grief, but I will see you again and you will rejoice, and no-one will take away your joy. [23]In that day you will no longer ask me anything. I tell you the truth, my Father will give you whatever you ask in my name. [24]Until now you have not asked for anything in my name. Ask and you will receive, and your joy will be complete.

[25]'Though I have been speaking figuratively, a time is coming when I will no longer use this kind of language but will tell you plainly about my Father. [26]In that day you will ask in my name. I am not saying that I will ask the Father on your behalf. [27]No, the Father himself loves you because you have loved me and have believed that I came from God. [28]I came from the Father and entered the world; now I am leaving the world and going back to the Father.'

[29]Then Jesus' disciples said, 'Now you are speaking clearly and without figures of speech. [30]Now we can see that you know all things and that you do not even need to have anyone ask you questions. This makes us believe that you came from God.'

[31]'You believe at last!' Jesus answered. [32]'But a time is coming, and has come, when you will be scattered, each to his own home. You will leave me all alone. Yet I am not alone, for my Father is with me.

[33]'I have told you these things, so that in me you may have peace. In this world you will have trouble. But take heart! I have overcome the world' (John 16:17-33).

They needed to focus on Jesus and his provision for them. Looking over the whole section from 15:1-16:33 we see how Jesus encouraged them and helped them get their focus right. Let's see how towards the end of chapter 16 Jesus summarised all that he had said and gave them all the assurance they needed in order to see straight and cope with the future. What they needed we need too, if we are to keep our spiritual balance.

1. They needed the assurance that Jesus cares for and provides for his disciples (16:33).

Jesus told the disciples that in this world they will face troubles of various kinds (*lit.* 'pressures'). But even in tribulation they could know his peace, they could be cheerful! They could, in the language of a popular current film, be a 'Braveheart'! You see, Jesus would be with them by his Spirit, ministering his peace and his presence. He would not leave them nor forsake them. He would strengthen and enable them. Their experience would not be as orphans (14:18). He assured them that he would continue to care for them and would provide all they needed to have uplifted hearts. All this they were to prove, and we can prove it too if we keep our eyes focused on Jesus and his caring provision for his disciples.

2. They needed the assurance that the absence of Jesus is not final (16:20ff.).

We will look at this passage in more detail in the last chapter of this book, but for the moment notice that Jesus told the disciples that he would see them after the Resurrection. When they would realise that he had risen from the dead, and that that event was the vindication of all that Jesus said he was and all that he came to do on the Cross for them, then no-one would be able to take away their joy (16:22). They would see him again. He is the conqueror of death.

Set in the wider context of these chapters there is a great truth here. The physical absence of Jesus from his disciples is never final! One day we will see him face to face. He will take us to be with him in his Father's house for ever! (14:3). In the meantime, he has given us 'another Comforter' to be with us as our companion 'for ever'. Death can be so final, but the death of Jesus makes it possible for us to spend eternity with him! So the absence of Jesus physically is never final for his disciples.

3. They needed the assurance that Jesus is the Victor over all his enemies (16:33).
They needed to know they were on the winning side! That is precisely the assurance that Jesus gave them in verse 33, and his resurrection would prove that beyond all doubt. I like the comment of Don Carson on this verse: 'Jesus' point is that by his death he has made the world's opposition pointless and beggarly.'[6] His death was not the final sad end to a great life, but the moment of his glory as he fulfilled on the Cross God's redemptive purpose for all his disciples.

The disciples' faith might have been slow and feeble but it was real (16:30, 31). In the challenges they would face they needed to know on whose side they were and if that side would win! Jesus gave them that assurance and he gives it to his disciples today also! What great and wonderful good news!

---

6. D. A. Carson, *Gospel According to John*, IVP, 1991, p. 550.

These truths sum up the encouragement of this whole section. Jesus promises his disciples his personal *care*, *companionship*, and final *conquest*. In the pressures of living in our lost world he promises us the same too! How encouraging!

The Last Prayer
(John 17)

In John 17, we read what might be called a 'final' prayer of Jesus for the disciples and for all those who would believe in him through their message. In some respects, as one person has written, this prayer is a summary of the entire Gospel of John. It is a magnificent prayer, this prayer of the Lord Jesus. It has been called the 'high-priestly' prayer of Jesus, or his prayer of 'consecration'. Westcott called it the 'consecration of Jesus to his death and glorification'[1] as well as a prayer for the disciples to carry on his mission to the world.

The prayer divides neatly into three sections: Jesus prays (1) for himself (verses 1-5); (2) for the disciples (verses 6-19); (3) for all believers down the ages, looking forward to every member of the church of Jesus Christ (verses 20-26).

1. His prayer for himself (17:1-5)
Right at the beginning, Jesus says, 'Father, the time has come; glorify your Son' (verse 1). At a first look, it seems strange that the first person that Jesus prays for is himself. Do you know the story of the middle-aged spinster, who prayed somewhat desperately, 'Lord, I wouldn't pray anything for myself, but please send my mother a son-in-

---

1. B. F Westcott, *The Gospel According to St. John*, John Murray, 1908.

After Jesus said this, he looked towards heaven and prayed: 'Father, the time has come. Glorify your Son, that your Son may glorify you. [2]For you granted him authority over all people that he might give eternal life to all those you have given him. [3]Now this is eternal life: that they may know you, the only true God, and Jesus Christ, whom you have sent. [4]I have brought you glory on earth by completing the work you gave me to do. [5]And now, Father, glorify me in your presence with the glory I had with you before the world began.

[6]'I have revealed you to those whom you gave me out of the world. They were yours; you gave them to me and they have obeyed your word. [7]Now they know that everything you have given me comes from you. [8]For I gave them the words you gave me and they accepted them. They knew with certainty that I came from you, and they believed that you sent me. [9]I pray for them. I am not praying for the world, but for those you have given me, for they are yours. [10]All I have is yours, and all you have is mine. And glory has come to me through them. [11]I will remain in the world no longer, but they are still in the world, and I am coming to you. Holy Father, protect them by the power of your name – the name you gave me – so that they may be one as we are one. [12]While I was with them, I protected them and kept them safe by that name you gave me. None has been lost except the one doomed to destruction so that Scripture would be fulfilled.

[13]'I am coming to you now, but I say these things while I am still in the world, so that they may have the

full measure of my joy within them. [14]I have given them your word and the world has hated them, for they are not of the world any more than I am of the world. [15]My prayer is not that you take them out of the world but that you protect them from the evil one. [16]They are not of the world, even as I am not of it. [17]Sanctify them by the truth; your word is truth. [18]As you sent me into the world, I have sent them into the world. [19]For them I sanctify myself, that they too may be truly sanctified.

[20]'My prayer is not for them alone. I pray also for those who will believe in me through their message, [21]that all of them may be one, Father, just as you are in me and I am in you. May they also be in us so that the world may believe that you have sent me. [22]I have given them the glory that you gave me, that they may be one as we are one: [23]I in them and you in me. May they be brought to complete unity to let the world know that you sent me and have loved them even as you have loved me.

[24]'Father, I want those you have given me to be with me where I am, and to see my glory, the glory you have given me because you loved me before the creation of the world.

[25]'Righteous Father, though the world does not know you, I know you, and they know that you have sent me. [26]I have made you known to them, and will continue to make you known in order that the love you have for me may be in them and that I myself may be in them' (John 17:1-26).

law!'? We have been schooled not to pray for ourselves first and foremost. So why is it that right at the commencement of this magnificent prayer we find Jesus praying for himself?

1. He prays for the Father's glory

Jesus' first request to the Father is, 'Glorify your Son that your Son may glorify you.' The glory of God is that which reveals who God really is, it is the manifestation of his character. Marcus Rainsford, who wrote a magnificent book on John 17, defined glory as 'the outward shining of the inward being of God'.[2]

There are lots of nuances regarding 'glory' in John 17. But to help us understand it, consider verses 6 and 22: 'I have revealed you to those whom you gave to me out of the world'; 'I have given them the glory that you gave me.' In a very real sense, that is two different ways of saying the same thing. The glory of God, the outshining of God, displays who God really is; and Jesus as the unique Son of God, the second Person of the Trinity, reveals God. Remember that key verse: 'No-one has ever seen God, but God the only Son, who was at the Father's side, has made him known' (John 1:18). Jesus has revealed God, he has narrated him.

What comes through so often in John's Gospel is that the Father's glory is wrapped up with the Son's glory; that they are bound up together, and if we are to honour the Father, then we have to honour the Son. There is no way to honour God, to know who he really is, to encounter his glory, except through his Son. The glorification of the Son entails the glorification of God the Father. Jesus

---

2. Marcus Rainsford, *Our Lord Prays for His Own*, Moody Press, 1950.

knew what would bring glory to God, what would display God, what would reveal him to be who he is – the loving, holy, all-powerful, wonderful Creator-God, who has become our Redeemer. Jesus knew that his obedience, not just through his life on earth, but his obedience unto death, would reveal the glory of God.

Actually it is the Cross of the Lord Jesus that displays supremely the glory of God. John Calvin put it better than anyone else I have read:

> 'For in the cross of Christ, as in a splendid theatre, the incomparable goodness of God is set before the whole world. The glory of God shines indeed in all creatures on high and below, but never more brightly than in the cross.'[3]

So, when Jesus prays that the Father may glorify the Son, it is a moving expression of his own willingness to obey his Father even unto death.

2. *He prays for his chosen people (17:2, 3)*

'For you granted him authority over all people that he might give eternal life to all those you have given him. Now this is eternal life: that they may know you, the only true God, and Jesus Christ, whom you have sent.' He prays for his own people. It was for them that he had come.

Jesus as the eternal Son of God has always had divine authority. But that is not the authority he refers to here. Jesus has also been given special authority by the Father to carry out the divine purpose of giving eternal life to those who would love him and trust him. If you connect the 'may' of verse 1 (that your Son may glorify you) with

---

3. John Calvin, *Commentary on John*, Vol. 2.

the 'might' of verse 2 (he might give eternal life), you will see my point. There is a connection between Jesus bringing glory to the Father and his giving eternal life to his people.

Eternal life is beautifully defined by the Lord Jesus as 'knowing God and Jesus Christ whom he has sent'. It begins with a personal relationship with the living God, it means coming to know the Creator and Sustainer of the universe, the invisible God, through his Son, the Lord Jesus Christ. To know him and to be brought into relationship with him is to have eternal life.

3. He prays for himself (17:4-5)

Jesus then consecrated himself for this great task that lay ahead: 'I have brought you glory on earth by completing the work you gave me to do. And now, Father, glorify me in your presence with the glory I had with you before the world began.' Jesus, in verse 4, was not only referring to his ministry up until this point, but looking forward to what he would be enabled to do; looking forward to the completion of his work; looking forward to that point where he could cry on the Cross, 'It is finished!' What God had sent him to do, he would complete. And so he prays (verse 5) that the Father would clothe him with glory and splendour, and give him back that which was his by right – the divine glory he had shared throughout eternity with the Father in heaven. Heaven was, and now is, where he is seen most fully as the One he really is.

2. He prays for his disciples (17:6-19)

First of all, Jesus says they *belonged to the Father from eternity* (6b). God knows those who are his and has planned their redemption from before time began. He determined to have them for his own possession. He knew them by name and set about redeeming them in his great and grand purposes. He took the initiative and *reached out* in love (see John 6:44). Behind their choice of God is his choice of them; behind their coming to know him is his initiative to save them. God has reached out to redeem.

Secondly, not only has God reached out to them, but Jesus has *revealed* God to them: 'I have revealed you to those whom you gave to me out of the world' (17:6). Christianity is not a faith for those who are wiser than others, because by their cleverness they understand the truth. Christianity is a revelation-faith, where God has taken the initiative to reveal himself.

Recently I was talking to a very determined police-woman with whom I had had many debates and arguments about the things of God before she became a believer. On one Sunday morning she said to me, 'I don't understand why I have never seen it before; how glorious it is, how wonderful is the love of God.' And her face showed it!

God, through his Son, by his Spirit, reveals himself to us, opens our minds that we might understand the things of God, bends our wills to be submissive to his saving truth, and warms our hearts by it.

Thirdly, Jesus *rescued* the disciples from a rebellious and lost world. The disciples may have been bewildered and confused, fearful and troubled, but their faith was real, and owned by Jesus. Describing them he said: 'They now know that everything you have given me comes from you. For I gave them the words you gave me and they accepted them. They knew with certainty that I came from you, and they believed that you sent me' (verses 7 and 8). They accepted that Jesus was the Truth. On one occasion, when the crowd could not take what Jesus was teaching and decided to stop following him, he said to the disciples, 'You do not want to leave too, do you?' And Peter replied, 'Lord, to whom shall we go? You have the words of eternal life' (John 6:67-68). They accepted his words and trusted in him. Their faith may have been shaky, but it was real. In his prayer here, these disciples are acknowledged by Jesus.

Down the centuries there have been two tendencies in the professing church of Jesus Christ. There has, on the one hand, been the monastic tendency, the tendency to isolation from the world, to try and build walls around ourselves to isolate ourselves from the effects of a world in rebellion against God. Martin Luther, who attempted to live a monastic life, discovered that the problem was not just outside, it was in his own heart.

There is also an evangelical Protestant equivalent of that kind of monastic withdrawal. It practises an isolationism from the world that is separatism in the wrong sense: a withdrawal from any involvement with unbelievers. Sometimes I think that the timing of some church services helps maintain rather than challenge this isolation. I belong to a denomination that has early morning communion services. I remember a lady saying to me: 'I love coming to the early morning communion service, because I don't have to have anything to do with anybody else in this church. I don't even have to talk to you. I only have to shake your hand!' I know what she meant, but it was somewhat isolationist, even in relation to other Christians! But it is also true that Christians can end up with a whole circle of Christian friends, and withdraw from the world. They pray for the evangelistic effort, but have nobody to evangelise!

But if, on the one hand there is a danger of monastic withdrawal, on the other hand there is a libertine over-identification with the world, a losing of our distinctiveness and witness, a blurring of the edges, so that we become indistinguishable from the world.

Jesus, of course, knew what to pray for. And it is not surprising in the light of those two tendencies to see what Jesus prayed.

He prays first of all for *protection* for the disciples, 'I will remain in the world no longer, but they are still in the world, and I am coming to you. Holy Father, protect them by the power of your name – the name you gave me – so that they may be one as we are one' (verse 11). There are two ways of reading this verse. The New International Version says '*by* the power of your name'. I prefer to have it read: '*in* your name'. God's Name actually tells us what he is like, who he is, what are his concerns. Jesus is asking that they would be protected by being kept faithful to his revelation of the truth. If we apply this to ourselves, it means being protected by being kept faithful to the Word of God, the written revelation that testifies to the Living Word, the Lord Jesus.

He prays for protection for them from the insidious influences and outlook of a world that is hostile to the things of God (17:14). As we have seen already, when Christians stand for Jesus Christ the world will not like it. Sometimes we will be very unpopular if we stand for Christ. The pressures of the world are very considerable. The outlook of the world, the popular mind-set, is insidious. It hits us constantly from the media: television, radio, magazines, newspapers; we are constantly barraged by it. Jesus prays for protection for the disciples from the world.

And he prays for protection from the evil one (17:15), who has already been described in 16:11 as the prince of this world who orchestrates the rebellion of the sinful human heart. Peter was later to describe him as the one who 'prowls around like a roaring lion, looking for someone to devour' (1 Peter 5:8). I think Satan is rather like the dinosaurs of *Jurassic Park*: doomed but jolly dangerous if you get near them! Satan, though defeated by Calvary, still is very dangerous.

Also implied is that the disciples needed protection from frail human nature. 'Keep them safe. Give them my joy,' says Jesus. 'Keep them trusting, keep them in your Name. Keep them against the background of the frailness of the human heart.'

But notice that Jesus does not pray that they may be taken out of the world, but that they may be kept faithful in the world: 'My prayer is not that you take them out of the world...' (17:15). The purpose of Jesus is not that his disciples would have the equivalent of a perpetual Bible Convention with no more hassle of work, no more problems with unbelievers, no more difficulties. It is not that his disciples should live on a spiritual mountain top week in week out. Yes, we need such times to recharge our spiritual batteries and be encouraged. But Jesus' purpose for us is that we go back into a lost world and live there for him. His prayer is that we live among people as salt and light. Jesus is not praying for monastic isolationism of any kind, but rather for an involvement in the world:

'As you sent me into the world, I have sent them into the world' (17:18).

Not only does he pray for their protection, he also prays for their *purification*: 'Sanctify them by the truth; your word is truth' (17:17). If one tendency of Christians is to become monastic and isolationist, the other tendency, as we have noted above, is to become libertine and indistinct. It is obedience to God's truth that will keep them and us. Jesus prays that the disciples may be sanctified, that they may be set apart, that they may be in the world, among unbelievers, but that they may keep their distinctiveness.

As Christians, how many unbelievers do we really know? How many are we making friends with? As we get involved with them, showing them Christ's love, sharing with them the good news of the gospel, which is the only answer to the lostness and bewilderment of our world, we have the assurance that Jesus prays we might remain distinctive, as he prayed for the disciples here.

Lastly, and very preciously, he prays that they may not only be protected and purified, but that they may be *glorified* (17:24). The only want on his prayer list is that he wants them to be with him and to share his glory. In a sense, if I may put it this way, heaven will not be complete unless those whom he has redeemed are there to share it with him! How lovely that is!

3. His prayer for the church (17:20-26)
Jesus prays for oneness in fellowship amongst the disciples down the years: 'My prayer is not for them alone. I pray also for those who will believe in me through their message, that all of them may be one, Father, just as you

are in me, and I am in you' (verses 20-21). This oneness must come through the apostolic witness to the revelation of God in his Son, that is, the Scriptures. I can see four aspects of this unity.

1. Oneness in apostolic truth

The church in every generation is tied to the apostolic witness to the revelation of God in Jesus Christ. Those who find eternal life, who come to know God, will be those who believe in the apostolic testimony to the truth. The church is forever tied to the foundation of the whole superstructure which is the apostles' and prophets' testimony to the revelation of God in the Lord Jesus Christ (Ephesians 2:20). What other Christ do we know than the Christ revealed in the written Word of God, i.e. the Bible? We are not free to adjust New Testament teaching. When the church moves away from this apostolic testimony, it becomes foolish. Such departure from the truth prevents people coming to know God. It is not up to us in our sinful arrogance to try to adjust or improve the revelation of God in Christ. Jesus prayed for oneness in apostolic truth.

2. Oneness in apostolic experience of Christ

Look at verse 26: 'I have made you known to them, and will continue to make you known in order that the love you have for me may be in them, and that I myself may be in them.' Just as he had revealed God to the disciples gathered around him, he will, by his Spirit, reveal himself to those who will believe in him through the apostolic message preached down the centuries. And notice he will go on revealing himself. It will not be limited to our conversion when we were brought into the family of God, but Jesus, through his Spirit from his Word, will continue to reveal more about God to his faithful disciples. Oneness in apostolic experience is an ongoing and growing experience of God and his Son.

3. Oneness in apostolic destiny

His people are cleansed for eternal life, for an endless personal relationship with God. Thomas Manton the Puritan wrote, 'When Christ made his will, heaven is one of the legacies which he bequeathed to us. This was his last will and testament, heaven is ours, a legacy left by Christ.' [4]

4. Oneness in apostolic mission

His followers are sent into the world to bear witness, to carry the apostolic testimony to every generation, so that they too may believe.

Fundamentally, the prayer of Jesus in John 17 has been answered and goes on being answered as people come to know him and as he reveals himself to them.

Have you ever noticed the order of fellowship in 1 John 1:3: 'We proclaim to you what we have seen and heard, so that you also may have fellowship with us. And our fellowship is with the Father and his Son, Jesus Christ.' We might have expected the order to be, first of all, fellowship with the Father and his Son and then fellowship with apostolic believers. But that is not what John wrote. He understood the point of the prayer in John 17! First, the disciples needed to have fellowship in receiving

---

4. T. Manton, *An Exposition of John 17*, Sovereign Grace Book Club, p. 405.

the apostolic testimony to Jesus Christ; and as they received that apostolic testimony, they were brought into fellowship with the Father and his Son. The church, throughout its existence on earth, is meant to be tied to the apostolic testimony.

But what conclusions can we draw from this magnificent prayer of Jesus?

Firstly, as God's children we have *security*. He permanently protects us. We have a Saviour who will never give up on us, who keeps those whom he has saved (see John 10:28). Secondly, our *sanctification* has begun and one day will be brought to completion (17:17). The Holy Spirit works in us to make us holy, sanctifying us and setting us apart so that we live distinctively for Jesus and bear witness to the apostolic testimony about him, as we show changed lives and lifestyle in a lost world. And we are assured that one day this process will be complete when we get to heaven: 'For those whom he foreknew, he also predestined to be conformed to the likeness of his Son' (Romans 8:29). Thirdly, we have *glorification* guaranteed. Heaven has been given to us as a legacy. What Jesus wants above all else is for those whom God sent him to redeem to spend eternity with him, to see and share his glory. The Spirit is ever committed to deepening our security, our sanctification and our sense of destiny.

These three benefits contribute to the oneness I referred to earlier in the chapter. I like the way Don Carson describes this oneness in his comments on verses 21 and 23:

Although the unity envisaged in this chapter is not institutional, this purpose clause at the end of verse 21 shows beyond all shadow of doubt that the unity is meant to be observable. It is not achieved by hunting enthusiastically for the lowest common theological denominator, but by common adherence to the apostolic gospel, by love that is joyfully self-sacrificing, by undaunted commitment to the shared goals of the mission with which Jesus' followers have been charged, by self-conscious dependence upon God himself for life and fruitfulness. It is a unity necessarily present and at least *in nuce* (essentially) among genuine believers; it is a unity that must be brought to perfection.[5]

Jesus prayed in verse 23: 'I in them, and you in me. May they be brought to complete unity to let the world know that you sent me and have loved them even as you have loved me.' His disciples are to display unity together in a common purpose, in a common belief, in a common mission. That unity of love and commitment to the apostolic testimony to Christ and that shared joyful commitment to the mission that Jesus gives to his church, is something that will make a lost world stand up and take notice. Unity in love and in truth will convince the world.

But the unity that God has given, the unity for which Jesus prayed here in this magnificent prayer for all his children, the unity that we see across the world in real believers, that unity is there. Isn't it wonderful to go to other continents, to change cultures, to come into different situations, and to find a unity in Jesus Christ between those who really believe in him and submit to the truth of God's Word? Praise him! Hallelujah! His prayer has been answered! There is a bond, there is a unity, but that unity is still to be brought to completion.

Ephesians 4 mentions two unities: 'unity in the Spirit' (verse 3) which we are to keep, and 'unity in the faith'

---

5. D. A. Carson, *Gospel According to John*, 1991, p.568.

which we are to reach (verse 13). In other words, we are to grow in our understanding of the truth and become more unified in our commitment to God's revelation and submissiveness to it, while making every effort to keep the unity of the Spirit. The unity that bonds real believers together, and has been given to us in answer to Christ's prayer, is a unity that is to be observed in a lost world. It requires hard work for it to be kept; it is to be maintained and it is to be brought to perfection. It is not to be hindered; Jesus prayed for it. Unity is something to be safeguarded and deepened.

When I was a student training for the ministry, I was part of a mission team. I was invited to preach at another evangelical church near the one I was based at. I arrived just after ten o'clock for the 10.30 service. The curate, the assistant minister, arrived at 10.15, the vicar arrived at 10.27. For the twelve minutes before the vicar arrived the curate did nothing other than criticise him, and for the last three minutes before we went into the service, the vicar did nothing other than criticise his curate! And that was an evangelical church, in which they would have both signed the same theological basis of faith. It was a communion service, and the vicar was at one end of the communion table, and the curate was at the other, and they read the words: 'Ye that do truly and earnestly repent ye of your sins and are in love and charity with your neighbours ...'. Do you know what I learned after the service? That the vicar and the curate had only spoken about essential business for two years! What an absolute disgrace!

If we earnestly want to have the prayer of Jesus answered in our church life and in our relationships with other Christians, let us deal with 'clouds' that come between us and those whom God has given us in his family. How foolish it is to let rifts happen among real Christian people! Yes, we won't agree about everything, but let's unite around the essentials of the apostolic gospel and the apostolic truth.

Of course there are real problems with churches which do not believe apostolic truth. That is a different issue! But with those who do believe the essentials of the gospel, let us work to keep the unity of the faith. Let us do everything to make sure that there is a visible unity of mission and purpose.

My brothers and sisters, it is important that this evangelical unity, this gospel unity (for that is what the word 'evangelical' means), might be safeguarded in our churches and between our churches. It is the concern of Jesus, it is the prayer of Jesus, that this unity may be seen, that it may be displayed, that it may be deepened. As I worked on this chapter, I have had cause as I prayed through it, to thank God for Conventions and every such thing that brings real believers together. There needs to be an *observable* unity amongst real believers, doesn't there? 'That the world may see and believe' (verses 21 and 23). God forgive us our preoccupation sometimes with secondary things. And God grant us that growing unity in a commitment to the apostolic truth and unity of the Spirit that a lost world needs to see.

SECTION 5

Lasting Joy

14

Christian Joy

In this chapter I want us to look at a great theme which runs throughout the Upper Room discourses. It is the theme of lasting joy. I came across a comment recently: 'Joy is faith dancing: peace is faith resting.'

One thing that marked out the observable experience of Jesus was the joy that stemmed from his relationship with his Father. That same joy was something which Jesus wanted his disciples to experience for themselves. But how could that be?

As we have seen, the immediate background of these chapters is the 'troubled hearts' of the disciples at the prospect of the departure of the one they loved, and their fear that their faith would be under great pressure. So Jesus encourages them not to be troubled, but rather to realise what he was doing for them. They needed to trust him. Things were not outside his control, rather God's purpose was being fulfilled and he was opening the way to heaven for them (14:1).

So he taught them key truths so that they might withstand the pressure of the traumatic events of Good Friday and the first Easter. 'I have told you all this to guard you against the breakdown of your faith' (16:1, New English Bible). So these chapters are designed to prevent a faith breakdown!

Is it possible to know joy in distressing circumstances?

The answer of these chapters is a resounding yes! Christians will not be removed from their fair share of heartache and heartbreak; circumstances for them will sometimes be hard and challenging, but there is a joy they can know despite the problems they may be facing. That is good news!

Has this proved true in Christian experience down the years? It has indeed!

I think of a woman whom I had the privilege of leading to Christ a few years ago. Recently she was diagnosed as having terminal cancer, and given only a short time to live. I went to see her in hospital, worried about how she would be taking the news. I went to encourage her and to cheer her up. Yes, she was sad at the news and the prospect of leaving the family which she so loved, and concerned for her husband and grown-up children as to how they would cope.

But there was a joy about her and a confidence that 'her life and times' were in the hands of a Saviour who loved her and would not fail her or her family. I went to cheer her up, but she cheered me up. And so it was until her death. Despite the tears there was joy and there was hope.

That story could be repeated countless times. In the years that I have been a minister of the gospel, it has been my privilege to see similar situations so many times, and indeed to know something of the same experience of joy in adversity. There is a quality of Christian joy which is unlike anything else, and is seen only in real believers.

Before we turn to look at the secret of the joy that Jesus wanted his disciples to experience, let us acknowledge another not so happy reality. There is a lack of joy in our churches at times. Not that joy is always having a cheesy grin! Too often, however, the church is not known for its joy.

Recently I was listening to a phone-in on the radio in which a caller in describing her weekend mentioned a visit to church. The response of the radio interviewer was sarcastic: 'I bet that was a joyful experience for you.' Sadly, that would be the impression many people would be left with by a visit to some churches. Why should this be, if Jesus wants his disciples to experience his joy, and indeed to manifest it in their lives? We need to take seriously the encouragement to make our joy 'complete'.

How then are the disciples to experience this joy day by day? What is the pathway to it and on what is it based? These are important questions for us and we need to take to heart the teaching of Jesus here. Further, in his high priestly prayer for the disciples recorded in chapter 17, Jesus prays for them to have this joy, and reveals that he has taught them 'so that they may have the full measure of my joy within them' (17:14).

Let us look then at what the loving Saviour teaches the first disciples and us in these chapters. Basically he says three things that are essential for experiencing joy: knowledge, obedience and prayer. We will look at each requirement.

1. There is joy in knowledge (16:17-23a)

Jesus informed the disciples that their grief at his departure would be turned to joy when they saw him again! He was referring to his resurrection. Already he had told them: 'I will not leave you as orphans; I will come to you' (14:18). Then they would realise that their worst fears had been groundless, and that Jesus had risen from the dead.

Then their joy would be impossible to take away.

Jesus, to describe their situation, used the picture of a woman giving birth to a baby (16:21). The pain of delivery gives way to the joy of the new arrival! So the disciples would experience pain, but when they realised that their Saviour was alive, all that pain would be forgotten in the joy of his resurrection.

I well remember when my wife gave birth to our first child, our daughter Jessica. She had a hard labour – some twenty-one and a half hours. We saw through three shifts at the hospital and then back again to the first! It seemed that the birth would never happen, and I was anxious about my wife's constant pain. Jessica was finally born, at about 4 am, to much joy. After the delightful period of rejoicing in our lovely new arrival and making the necessary joyful phone calls, I went home.

I registered the baby first thing at 9 am and returned to the ward as soon as I was allowed, which was 1 pm. With that male naïvety I expected my wife to look shattered and be worn out. Certainly I would have made a lot of it if it had been me going through all that pain! But there she was sitting up in bed, full of joy as she held our daughter in her arms! The meaning of these verses from the Upper Room came home to me in a fresh way.

The analogy that Jesus used is powerful and true. When the disciples discovered that he had risen, then their joy swallowed up their previous pain.

The resurrection was the vindication of all that Jesus had said and done. It was the acceptance by the Father of his sin-bearing atonement on our behalf. His work had been completed according to the Father's will. All that he said about himself and his mission had been true.

It is interesting that Peter, in the first recorded sermon after the resurrection, told his hearers that 'God raised him from the dead' (Acts 2:24). It was not that Jesus raised himself, but that God the Father raised Jesus as the vindication of all that he said and did. All that was necessary for the salvation of his people had been accomplished.

Notice too that Peter goes on to say in the same sermon: 'Nor did his body see decay' (Acts 2:31). Jesus had *physically* risen from the dead! It is not that the spirit of Jesus lives on, rather like the way some believe the spirit of Elvis Presley lives on in his music and in the effect that he still has on his fans. It is not that the spirit of Jesus lives on, with his bones still lying in a Palestinian tomb. Not a bit of it! The previous Bishop of Durham's explanation of the resurrection bears no similarity to Peter's account.

No, the resurrection of Jesus is much more than that! He is alive, and his resurrection has opened the gateway to heaven for us. He rose *totally*, so that we might one day rise totally, with new resurrection bodies, to be with him for ever. This is what enabled the early Christians to face persecution and death without fear. Their Lord was the Lord of life and death, and he would never forsake them, whatever life might bring. They had a sure hope in life and in death.

Christians do not follow a dead hero whose influence lives on in his writings alone. They follow a living Lord with whom they enjoy a living relationship, and whom they shall, one day, see face to face.

This knowledge is the ground of Christian joy. We feed on our knowledge of the truth as we get to know the teaching of the Bible, in order to understand our faith better. There is joy in knowledge.

2. There is joy in obedience (15:9-17)

As we have already seen, we need to bask in the love of God for us. We need to glory in it and rejoice because of it, and we need to let that gracious love kindle fresh love in our hearts for him. How is that love to be seen?

How is love for a marriage partner seen? Is it just in words, or is there more to it than that? It is true that many a marriage has been starved through a lack of loving words of appreciation and affection. Words are important, and too many wives complain about the lack of loving words from their husbands (it does so often seem to be men who are not so good in the words department). The right word can mean a lot at the right time.

But love for a partner is seen not just in words but in actions. If we really love someone we will care about what pleases them. As I write this chapter, my wife is away, and I received through the post this morning a little card encouraging me to stick at it! I was encouraged.

Think of a parent/child relationship. It is true that a relationship between a father and son or a mother and daughter can be strained when obedience to the parent's wishes is neglected. This is especially the case when a good parent warns about something which is in the best interests of the child.

In that context, obedience is the best expression of love, for it reveals trust in the fact that the parent has the child's best interests at heart. Disregard of commands in that context definitely causes a cloud in an otherwise happy and stable relationship.

Jesus had been talking about remaining in his love (15:9). How are the disciples to remain in his love and so show themselves to be his trusting disciples? Jesus' answer is clear – by taking his words seriously through understanding from whom they come (15:7) and being obedient to those things that please him (15:10).

That is how we avoid a cloud in our relationship with Jesus, and indeed how we avoid danger to ourselves through our own folly. Obedience is the key to Christian living.

Jesus said: 'If you obey my commands, you will remain in my love, just as I have obeyed my Father's commands and remain in his love' (15:10). And he continued: 'I have told you this so that my joy may be in you and that your joy may be complete' (15:11). Obedience is the way to joy, and our joy will be incomplete in a corresponding measure to our disobedience.

It is increasingly important to register this point in a secular and godless society. Young Christians suffer many siren voices that encourage them away from God's way with the promise of pleasure and joy. And it is not only the young who are under pressure; pressures in business and from the media exert a powerful pull on all believers.

The world constantly encourages us to swallow the lie that disobedience to God's commands is the way of joy. Nothing could be further from the truth! The world's ways may bring temporary pleasures, but they leave various hangovers to face in subsequent days.

Obedience is the best expression of our trust in our Saviour's genuine love for us. Genuine obedience shows we believe that Jesus really has our best interests at heart.

How can we doubt that in the light of Calvary?

Have you noticed how miserable a wilfully disobedi-ent Christian is? Not in terms of their eternal standing before God, but in terms of their present experience, the most miserable people on earth are disobedient Chris-tians. God has given us a new nature with an inclination to follow him, and if we pull against that we will be miserable. Indeed, in this sense, far more miserable than an unbeliever!

I ask you as I ask myself, has God been putting his finger on some unresolved issue in your life recently? It might be a relationship, or a job, or an ambition. It might be the use of your time, or your talents, or your resources, or whatever. You know what God wants you to do, but you have been trying to avoid it. Obedience to God's Word is the way of joy!

In this passage, although Jesus is referring to all his commands, he especially singles out the command to 'love each other' in the Christian family (15:12, 17). So many problems are caused by the lack of forgiveness in the church and by unresolved issues between Christians. So often the work of God and the joy of believers are hindered by this lack. How can we hope to convince a lost world of the truth of what we stand for, if it is not seen in different relationships in the church? The lonely world longs to see real love somewhere – a love that is strong and unselfish and forgiving.

If we have experienced the love of Jesus to us, he calls us to reflect that same quality of love to all in the Christian family. It is the way of joy! We need more of this love to be seen in our fellowships and in our lives.

In short, if we disregard the commands of Jesus, we

will simply deny ourselves joy. There is a joy, from going the right way and doing the right thing, which is incomparable. Therefore, the desire to please the One who loves us should be uppermost in our minds and hearts.

Seek joy and you will never find it – follow Jesus and the by-product is joy!

3. There is joy in prayer (16:23b-28)

'Until now you have not asked anything in my name. Ask and you will receive, and your joy will be complete' (16:24).

Jesus encouraged the disciples to pray in his name, that is, in accordance with his character and his will. We cannot use the authority of his name to request that which is contrary to the revealed character of God or that which is against his revealed will for us in Holy Scripture.

Increasingly I come across people who have decided to do what the Bible forbids. Often they comment that they have thought long and hard about what they intend to do and have even prayed earnestly about it before coming to the conclusion to proceed! But we need to submit in prayer to his revealed will for our lives, for only then do we really pray in his name!

Prayer is a means of expression of our trust in our Father's will for us. It is in prayer that we show best our childlike trust and dependence on him.

Have you ever thought deeply about prayer? After all, God is omniscient, that is, he knows everything about everything. So if he knows what we need before we pray, and even knows how we will pray before we do, why bother to pray at all?

The answer of Jesus is that prayer is for the benefit of

his disciples. So often God withholds his hand until his people pray. He will seem to let his purposes be hindered by the lack of prayer. Why? Because God in his infinite goodness wishes to involve us in his eternal plans through prayer, and to increase our joy by doing so. Let me explain.

Suppose you pray regularly for someone in your family whom you care deeply about, say your brother. He desperately needs Christ, but you have just never been able to get through to him. But you have gone on praying and sometimes despaired of an answer.

Just imagine when he tells you that he had talked casually with someone on the Tube who was reading a Bible and who had given him a tract. Subsequently, unknown to you, he had bought a Bible, read some of it with interest, and gone along to the local church because of his growing attraction to Jesus. There he had been befriended by some people of his own age and been invited to a guest service, and as a result he had given his life to Christ. Imagine your joy when you hear that! God has answered your prayer, and you are overjoyed.

It is true that we may never see in this life the answer to some of our prayers. But God does want us to pray specifically in order that we may have the joy of seeing him work in answer to our prayers. He wants to build a relationship with us, and our joy will grow as we pray and see him at work. This is how our joy will be complete (16:24).

As we pray there will be answers – maybe not when we always wish, or in the way that we would like. Sometimes God says 'No' as well as 'Yes' or 'Not yet'. I thank God now that he didn't answer some of my earlier prayers as a young Christian! I'm so glad that some relationships did not develop in the way I hoped and prayed they would! However, if we pray, there will be answers and there will be increasing joy and encouragement, and we will get to know God better.

Earlier, I said that sometimes our churches did not reflect the joy that they should. Could this be because, generally speaking, the prayer meeting is the most poorly attended meeting, even in the liveliest churches? How is it that, in the busyness of life, the first thing to be squeezed out in our lives is prayer? Is it any wonder that we are lacking the joy that we should have?

I heard of a survey some time ago which concluded that Christians pray on average for one minute a day. Fear not, pastors were better – about one minute and thirty seconds! A more recent survey of ministers concluded that they spent about four minutes a day in prayer! Of course, it is not the length that matters, but the reality of the relationship with God in pouring out our hearts to him. Indeed we are to have, at all times, the kind of relationship with God that shares all of each day with him.

But these surveys are a frightening barometer of life among Christians in Britain. Is it any wonder that so many churches are declining? If we are not praying for conversions, it is less likely that we will see them happen. If we are not praying for the lost, do we really care for them?

I once worked in a church that was just becoming a fully evangelical church. The turning-point was when various 'prayer triplets' were organised, and real believers began to pray specifically. ('Prayer triplets' is a scheme where three people meet once a week to pray for as long as they wish, be it five minutes or two hours. They pray for one another's concerns and also for three friends each who don't know the Lord.)

So then, there is joy in prayer, and there will be a corresponding lack of joy when we do not pray. The most joyful churches are the praying churches!

Let me end this chapter by returning to where I began. Jesus says in John 17:13 that he said things to his disciples and prayed for them so that they may have the full measure of his joy within them. Therefore we need to take to heart what he teaches in these chapters about (1) the knowledge of his resurrection, (2) comprehensive obedience to his commands, and (3) regular prayer. These three things are necessary requirements for our joy to be complete, and that is his desire for us.

Postscript

As we think back on these magnificent chapters in John's Gospel, we see a Saviour who displayed his love for his disciples, gave them an example of how to live, took the time and the trouble to answer their questions, warned them, encouraged them, gave them a job to do and the equipment to do it, and promised to be with them by his Spirit. How he loved and prayed for his disciples when the focus of his attention might well have been his suffering and death the next day! But then his death was the reason for which he came, and it was to open the way to his Father's house for his disciples. Here we see a Saviour who is focused on the real needs of his disciples. A Saviour who loves them to death and beyond! Here is a Saviour who loves his 'friends' with an amazing love.

Jesus loves and died for his disciples in every age. Do you know this wonderful Saviour? Are you walking with him and trusting in him day by day? Are your heart and mind focused on the precious promises he makes to his own children in these passages? Is obedience to his wishes and commands your heart's desire? He loves his disciples with such a love, and he always has their best interests uppermost in his mind. How foolish we are to spend any time away from him who loves us so! He is the one in whom is found real life, eternal life.

This book comes with the prayer that its pages may, with the help of the Holy Spirit, draw you with wonder and worship to a fresh appreciation of the love of Jesus for you, and encourage you to abide in him, and to learn well that apart from him you can do nothing.

> Love so amazing, so divine
> Demands my soul, my life, my all.

Bibliography

George R. Beasley-Murray, *John*, Word Biblical Commentary, 1987.

F. F. Bruce, *The Gospel of John*, Eerdmans, 1992.

John Calvin, *John Volume 1 and 2,* Eerdmans and Paternoster.

D. A. Carson, *The Gospel According to John*, IVP, 1991.

Matthew Henry, *John*.

J. Ramsey Michaels, *John,* New International Biblical Commentary, Hendrickson/Paternoster, 1995.

Bruce Milne, *The Message of John* (Bible Speaks Today), IVP, 1993.

Leon Morris, *The Gospel According to John*, Marshall, Morgan & Scott, 1972.

Marcus Rainsford, *Our Lord Prays For His Own,* Chicago, Moody Press, 1950 (first published 1873).

J. C Ryle, *Expository Thoughts on the Gospel of John*, Vol. 3, James Clarke and Co. Ltd, 1969.

John Stott, *Christ the Liberator*, Hodder and Stoughton, 1972.

Merrill C. Tenney, *John*, (Expositors Bible Commentary) Zondervan, 1981.

Among other Bible Versions I found the paraphrase of Eugene H. Peterson *The Message* helpful – published by Navpress, 1993.

Study Questions

Chapter 1
1. What is it that brings ultimate glory to Jesus and the Father (John 13:31)?

2. How did most people's view of Messiah differ from Jesus' understanding of his role (Isaiah 42:1-4; 52:13-53:12)?

3. How are John 13 and Philippians 2:6-11 connected?

4. Is there a deeper meaning to Jesus' washing his disciples' feet than showing a pattern of humble behaviour (John 13:6-8)?

5. What was it the disciples needed before they could serve Jesus?

6. What is the antidote to spiritual dryness?

7. Above all else, what is Christianity?

Chapter 2

1. What does it mean to affirm Jesus as Lord (John 13:13)?

2. What is the basis of Christian unity (John 13:16)?

3. What kind of servants does Jesus want?

4. What kind of love did Jesus model?

5. To whom are we to show love?

6. Can you think of some modern-day equivalents of foot-washing?

7. What should be our motivation for loving (1 John 4:19)?

8. How will people know who the disciples of Jesus are (John 13:35)?

Chapter 3

1. How much control did Jesus have over the events in the Upper Room (John 13:3)?

2. How would the disciples know that what Jesus told them would really happen (John 13:19)?

3. When might hurt we have suffered become sin in our own lives?

4. How can we overcome the hurts we have received?

5. How can we maintain a right perspective on life?

6. How much control does Jesus have over the painful events in our lives?

Chapter 4 – No questions

Chapter 5
1. When does the real test of our commitment to Jesus come?

2. What perspective do we need in order to face the challenges of life (John 14:1-2)?

3. What did Jesus mean by the many rooms in his Father's house?

4. How did Jesus 'prepare a place' for the disciples in heaven?

5. Why could the disciples not follow Jesus to heaven immediately (John 13:36-37)?

Chapter 6
1. What is Jesus' answer to perplexity and confusion?

2. Why is Jesus *the* only way to the Father?

3. How is Jesus the only way to the Father?

4. What is it necessary to have to be assured of eternal life?

Chapter 7
1. What three things was Jesus revealing about his relationship to his Father when he spoke to Philip?

2. Do all roads lead to God? If not, why not?

3. What important things does Jesus say about himself in John 14:11-14?

4. What do you think Jesus meant by 'greater things' in John 14:12?

Chapter 8
1. To what authority do our opinions constantly need to be submitted?

2. What is the mark of a disciple who loves Jesus (John 14:23)?

3. Are there things you recognise in yourself in the responses of the four disciples to Jesus' statements in this portion of Scripture?

4. How is the Trinity revealed to believers?

Chapter 9

1. Whom do we need to first understand if we are to understand the Holy Spirit?

2. How does the Holy Spirit act as 'counsel for the defence' on our behalf?

3. What is the difference in experience of the Holy Spirit of those under the Old Covenant and those under the New Covenant (John 14:17)?

4. What answers does Jesus give to those with troubled hearts (John 14:1-4, 18)?

5. What does holiness in the life of a believer mean in practice?

6. How does the Holy Spirit teach us (John 14:26)?

7. How are the benefits of Christ's death ministered to us?

Chapter 10

1. What does the Holy Spirit delight to do (John 15:26)?

2. What must we have in order to know the Holy Spirit's power (John 15:27)?

3. What kind of people are filled with the Holy Spirit (Acts 4:29, 31)?

4. Why was it for their good that Jesus left his disciples (John 16:7)?

5. Of what will the Spirit convince and convict people?

6. What is the only way to be righteous before God?

7. What might the 'yet to come' things be to which Jesus referred in this passage, of which the Holy Spirit would tell the disciples?

Chapter 11

1. What is the evidence of *life* in a person (John 15:2)?

2. What is the fruit of the Spirit in our lives?

3. How will this fruit be demonstrated (John 13:35)?

4. What does 'abiding' or 'remaining' in Jesus mean (John 15:7)?

5. In what way is our dependence on Christ best expressed?

6. What does friendship with God mean?

7. What is the difference between being a servant and being a friend?

8. What gives believers a great sense of security (John 15:16)?

Chapter 12

1. In all the pressure of living in a rebellious world, what is it vital to remember (John 15:19)?

2. What kind of treatment can we expect from the world if we belong to Christ (John 15:21)?

3. What is the heart of sin (John 16:8, 9)?

4. What should be the only ground of accusation against us as Christians?

5. How should we act towards the professing church?

6. What assurances do we need if we are to keep our spiritual balance?

Chapter 13

1. How do we understand 'the glory of God'?

2. Where is the glory of God supremely displayed?

3. How does Jesus define eternal life?

4. What two tendencies should we avoid in our interaction with the non-believing world?

5. How is the unity Jesus prayed for to be worked out practically?

Chapter 14

1. How can we know joy in distressing circumstances?

2. What is essential for experiencing joy?

3. What was it about the resurrection that enabled the early Christians to face persecution and death without fear?

4. How are we to remain in the love of Jesus (John 15:7, 9, 10)?

5. What one factor is most likely to make us lose our joy?

6. Which command did Jesus single out as important for the Christian family?

7. How important is prayer with regard to our experience of joy?

Wallace Benn is married and has two children. He is Vicar of St. Peter's Church, Harold Wood, Essex. A regular Spring Harvest and Convention speaker, also a former Keswick Convention Council member, he is on the executive of Word Alive, a member of the Church of England Evangelical Council, and a council member of 'Reform'. His interests include supporting the Irish Rugby Union team and watching any kind of motorsport.